W0009318

The Poolbeg Book of
IRISH
BALLADS

SEAN McMAHON

POOLBEG

A Paperback Original
First published 1991 by
Poolbeg Press Ltd
Knocksedan House,
Swords, Co Dublin, Ireland

© Selection and introduction Sean McMahon 1991

Grateful thanks is due to Waltons Ltd for permission to
reprint "Down by the Glenside" and "Whack Fol the Diddle"
by Peader Kearney.

ISBN 1 85371 127 9

Cover photograph and design by Pomphrey Associates
Set by Richard Parfrey in ITC Stone 9/14
Printed by The Guernsey Press Ltd,
Vale, Guernsey, Channel Islands

The Patriot Game

A Squeeze of Orange

The Lighter Side

The Criminal Element

About the Country

Exiles' Laments

Songs of True Love (Mostly Sad)

Sports and Other Enthertainments

Introduction

Dictionaries define the ballad as: "originally a song accompany–
ing a dance, now a simple narrative poem intended to be sung."
That will cover most of the contents of this book and the
secondary definitions of "a popular song, often scurrilous,
referring to contemporary events or persons" or "a drawing-
room song usually sentimental" will cover them all. For most
people the word "ballad" meant, in the days of near literacy,
the cheap, badly-printed "broadsides" that were on sale at fairs
and hustings, or hawked round the doors by pedlars. These told
of famous deeds of bravery or self-sacrifice, of cruelty and ill-
treatment, of rapes and robberies and murders, of great feats of
sportsmanship and gargantuan feasts, and above all of person-
alities and events set in the region where the balladeer hoped
to sell them. They became in this way the poetry of the people,
the common muse, and since their shelf-life was brief they
relied for their persistence on quality and oral transmission.

Because of Ireland's distressful history there was never any
lack of high deeds and noble "hayroes" to stir the unmute and
inglorious Miltons to making songs. The largest section in this
book deals with those who tried to right Ireland's wrong. If one
should assemble all the patriotic ballads of the last two hundred the result would be a very fat book indeed. It was the
known popularity of the broadside that caused Thomas Davis,
that greatest of adult educators, to fill the pages of *The Nation*
with "literary" ballads that should tell vigorous stories of noble
Irish men and women and yet have a nationalistic message and
a bit of cheer for the long oppressed.

Love, too, usually sad and unrequited, or if requited followed
by long and sometimes permanent separation, was also a staple
of the ballad form. The number of bonny boys and blithe girls

that were sung about is great and with sound commercial sense; many were associated with local habitations, from Ballycastle to Bantry. It is noteworthy that these topographical songs were usually about individual girls —flowers of sweet Strabane and charming Belfast girls—while those dedicated to boys were usually in the plural and praised them for tolerated riot and rampage, from Mallow to Donnybrook and back again.

Not all of them were, as Davis put it, "sad and desponding." Those written before the black Forties had a liveliness never regained. Puritanism entered the Irish psyche and stayed there till the coming of Telefís Éireann and the paperback revolution. The comic ballads of the early nineteenth-century are vigorous still.

As ever with anthologies the compiler has to apologise in advance for omissions, though he should never do it for inclusions. The ballads printed here are only a selection from a extant treasury. To those who would have made other choices, I respectfully say, "You must make your own anthology; and the fact that you can means you don't need to."

The Patriot Game

O'DONNELL ABU

Michael Joseph McCann

Ballad written for The Nation *celebrating one of the glories of Ireland's past, the defeat by Red Hugh O'Donnell of Sir Conyers Clifford at Ballyshannon (the "Saimear" of the fourth line) on 1 August 1597.* Abu *is an abbreviation for* "Go Bua! *(To Victory!)*

Proudly the note of the trumpet is sounding,
Loudly the war-cries arise on the gale;
Fleetly the steed by Loch Suiligh is bounding,
To join the thick squadrons in Saimear's green vale,
On, every mountaineer,
Strangers to flight and fear,
Rush to the standards of dauntless Red Hugh!
Bonnought and gallowglass
Throng from each mountain pass!
On for old Erin—O'Donnell abu!

Princely O'Neill to our aid is advancing,
With many a chieftain and warrior clan;
A thousand proud steeds in his vanguard are prancing
'Neath the borders brave from the banks of the Bann—
Many a heart shall quail
Under its coat of mail,
Deeply the merciless foeman shall rue,
When on his ear shall ring,
Borne on the breeze's wing,
Tir-Conaill's dread war-cry—O'Donnell abu!

Wildly o'er Desmond the war-wolf is howling,
Fearless the eagle sweeps over the plain;
The fox in the streets of the city is prowling,
All, all who would scare them are banished or slain.
Grasp, every stalwart hand,
Hackbut and battle-brand,
Pay them all back the deep debt so long due;
Norris and Clifford well
Can Tir-Conaill tell—
Onward to glory—O'Donnell abu!

Sacred the cause that Clan-Conaill's defending,
The altars we kneel at, the homes of our sires;
Ruthless the ruin the foe is extending,
Midnight is red with the plunderers' fires!
On with O'Donnell then,
Fight the old fight again,
Sons of Tir Conaill, all valiant and true!
Make the false Saxon feel
Erin's avenging steel!
Strike for your country!—O'Donnell abu!

THE BATTLE EVE OF THE BRIGADE

Thomas Davis

Typical of the stirring stuff that Thomas Davis wrote for the earliest numbers of The Nation, intent upon his purpose to give the demoralised Irish back their country. The battle is not specified but it was certainly one of the engagements that characterised the dynastic European wars of the early eighteenth century when the Wild Geese and their successors fought in the armies of any of England's enemies. In the original the language-conscious Davis had written the fourth line of the second verse as "Where Sionainn and Bearbha and Abhain Dubh flow."

The mess-tent is full, and the glasses are set,
And the gallant Count Thomond is president yet:
The vet'ran arose, like an uplifted lance,
Crying—"Comrades, a health to the monarch of France!"
With bumpers and cheers they have done as he bade.
For King Louis is loved by the Irish Brigade.

"A health to King James," and they bent as they quaffed,
"Here's to George the Elector," and fiercely they laughed.
"Good luck to the girls we wooed long ago,
Where Shannon, and Barrow, and Blackwater flow,"
"God prosper old Ireland"—you'd think them afraid,
So pale grew the chiefs of the Irish Brigade.

"But, surely, that light cannot come from our lamp?
And that noise—are they all getting drunk in the camp?"
"Hurrah! boys, the morning of battle is come,
And the general's beating on many a drum."
So they rush from the revel to join the parade:
For the van is the right of the Irish Brigade.

They fought as they revelled, fast, fiery, and true,
And, though victors, they left on the field not a few:
And they, who survived, fought and drank as of yore,
But the land of their heart's hope they never saw more:
For in far foreign fields, from Dunkirk to Belgrade,
Lie the soldiers and chiefs of the Irish Brigade.

THE BOYS OF WEXFORD

Robert Dwyer Joyce

To the weary constitutional nationalists of the nineteenth century the rising of 1798 which woke Ireland from its long eighteenth-century sleep seemed in retrospect an incredibly heady experience. Certainly no other event generated more songs even though most of them weren't written until more than fifty years after the event. This is one of the most famous.

In comes the captain's daughter, the captain of the Yeos,
Saying, "Brave United man, we'll ne'er again be foes.
A thousand pounds I'll give you, and fly from home with thee,
And dress myself in man's attire, and fight for libertie!"
We are the boys of Wexford, who fought with heart and hand
To burst in twain the galling chain, and free our native land!

"I want no gold, my maiden fair, to fly from home with thee;
Your shining eyes will be my prize—more dear than gold to me.
I want no gold to nerve my arm to do a true man's part—
To free my land I'd gladly give the red drops from my heart."
We are the boys of Wexford, who fought with heart and hand
To burst in twain the galling chain, and free our native land!

And when we left our cabins, boys, we left with right good will,
To see our friends and neighbours that were at Vinegar Hill!
A young man from our ranks, a cannon he let go;
He slapt it into Lord Mountjoy—a tyrant he laid low!
We are the boys of Wexford, who fought with heart and hand
To burst in twain the galling chain, and free our native land!

We bravely fought and conquered at Ross, and Wexford town;
And, if we failed to keep them,'twas drink that brought us down.
We had no drink beside us on Tubberneering's day,
Depending on the long bright pike, and well it worked its way!
We are the boys of Wexford, who fought with heart and hand
To burst in twain the galling chain, and free our native land!

They came into the country our blood to waste and spill;
But let them weep for Wexford, and think of Oulart Hill!
'Twas drink that still betrayed us—of them we had no fear;
For every man could do his part like Forth and Shelmalier!
We are the boys of Wexford, who fought with heart and hand
To burst in twain the galling chain, and free our native land!

My curse upon all drinking! It made our hearts full sore;
For bravery won each battle, but drink lost ever more;
And if, for want of leaders, we lost at Vinegar Hill,
We're ready for another fight, and love our country still!
We are the boys of Wexford, who fought with heart and hand
To burst in twain the galling chain, and free our native land!

The Ballad of Henry Joy

Anonymous

*Fine ballad tribute to one of Belfast's rebel sons, dating from a time
when Belfast was a radical city.*

An Ulster man I am proud to be,
From the Antrim Glens I come,
Although I labour by the sea,
I have followed flag and drum.
I have heard the martial tramp of men,
I have watched them fight and die;
And it's well do I remember
When I followed Henry Joy.

I pulled my boat up from the sea,
I hid my sails away,
I hung my nets on a greenwood tree,
And I scanned the moonlit bay,
The Boys went out, and the Redcoats, too;
I kissed my wife goodbye,
And in the shade of the greenwood glad,
Sure I followed Henry Joy.

In Antrim Town the tyrant stood,
He tore our ranks with ball,
But with a cheer and a pike to clear,
We swept them o'er the wall.
Our pikes and sabres flashed that day,
We won, but lost, ah! why
No matter, lads, I fought beside,
And shielded Henry Joy.

Ah, lads, for Ireland's cause we fought
For home and sire we bled,
Tho' pikes were fed, still our hearts beat true,
And five to one lay dead,
But many a lassie mourned her lad,
And mother mourned her boy;
For youth was strong in that gallant throng,
Who followed Henry Joy.

In Belfast town they built a tree,
And the Redcoats mustered there;
I watched him come as the beat of the drum
Rolled out from the barrack square.
He kissed his sister, went aloft,
Then bade a last goodbye,
My soul he died, och, I turned and cried,
They had murdered Henry Joy.

BOOLAVOGUE

Patrick Joseph McCall

Ninety-eight ballad giving a fair summary of the campaign of the Wexford insurgent leader John Murphy. His church had been burned by the North Cork militia on 26 May and after some success in skirmishes he was defeated at Kilcomney on 26 June and was tortured and killed by yeomen that same day.

At Boolavogue, as the sun was setting,
O'er the bright May meadows of Shelmalier,
A rebel hand set the heather blazing
And brought the neighbours from far and near,
Then Father Murphy, from old Kilcormack,
Spurred up the rock with a warning cry;
"Arm! Arm!" he cried, "for I've come to lead you
For Ireland's freedom we fight or die."

He led us on 'gainst the coming soldiers,
And the cowardly yeomen we put to flight;
'Twas at the Harrow the boys of Wexford
Showed Bookey's regiment how men could fight.
Look out for hirelings, King George of England,
Search every kingdom where breathes a slave,
For Father Murphy of County Wexford
Sweeps o'er the land like a mighty wave.

We took Camolin and Enniscorthy,
And Wexford storming drove out our foes;
'Twas at Slieve Coillte our pikes were reeking
With the crimson stream of the beaten Yeos.
At Tubberneering and Ballyellis
Full many a Hessian lay in his gore;
Ah, Father Murphy, had aid come over
The green flag floated from shore to shore.

At Vinegar Hill, o'er the pleasant Slaney,
Our heroes vainly stood back to back;
And the Yeos at Tullow took Father Murphy
And burned his body upon the rack.
God grant your glory, brave Father Murphy,
And open Heaven to all your men;
The cause that called you may call to-morrow
In another fight for the Green again.

Kelly of Killanne

PJ McCall

Along with "Boolavogue" one of the great ballads of the Wexford insurrection and written by the same balladeer. Kelly was killed at the battle of New Ross on 5 June 1798.

"What's the news? What's the news? O my bold Shelmalier,
With your long-barrelled gun of the sea?
Say what wind from the sun blows his messenger here,
With a hymn of the dawn for the free?"
"Goodly news, goodly news, do I bring Youth of Forth
Goodly news shall you hear, Bargy man!
For the boys march at morn from the South to the North,
Led by Kelly, the Boy from Killanne!"

"Tell me who is that giant with the gold curling hair—
He who rides at the head of your band?
Seven feet is his height, with some inches to spare,
And he looks like a king in command!"
"Ah, my lads, that's the pride of the bold Shelmaliers,
'Mong our greatest of heroes, a man!—
Fling your beavers aloft and give three ringing cheers
For John Kelly, the Boy from Killanne!"

Enniscorthy's in flames, and old Wexford is won,
And the Barrow to-morrow we cross!
On a hill o'er the town we have planted a gun
That will batter the gateway of Ross!
All the Forth men and Bargy men march o'er the heath,
With brave Harvey to lead on the van;
But the foremost of all in the grim Gap of Death
Will be Kelly, the Boy from Killanne!

But the gold sun of freedom grew darkened at Ross,
And it set by the Slaney's red waves;
And poor Wexford, stript naked, hung high on a cross,
And her heart pierced by traitors and slaves!
Glory O! Glory O! to her brave sons who died,
For the cause of long down-trodden men!
Glory O! to Mount Leinster's own darling and pride—
Dauntless Kelly, the Boy from Killanne!

BILLY BYRNE OF BALLYMANUS

Anonymous

*A contemporary ballad of 1798 written for an audience who knew the facts.
Byrne was found guilty on the evidence of Thomas Reynolds, whose role as an
informer had been kept hidden till then. He was hanged on 25 July 1798.*

Come all ye brave United Men, I pray you lend an ear,
And listen to these verses I now will let you hear,
Concerning Billy Byrne, a man of great renown,
Who was tried and hanged at Wicklow town, a traitor to the Crown.

It was in the year of ninety-eight, we got reason to complain,
We lost our brave commander, Billy Byrne was his name;
He was taken to Dublin city and brought to Wicklow Jail,
And though we wished to free him, for him they'd take no bail.

When he was taken prisoner the lot against him swore
That he a Captain's title upon Mount Pleasant bore,
Before the King's grand army his men he did review
And with a piece of cannon marched on for Carrigue.

And when the trial was started, the informers they came in
There was Dixon, Doyle and Davis and likewise Bid Doolin
They thought it little scruple his precious blood to spill
Who never robbed nor murdered nor to any man did ill.

It would melt your heart with pity how these traitors did explain
That Byrne worked the cannon on Arklow's bloody plain,
They swore he worked the cannon and headed the pikemen,
And near the town of Gorey killed three loyal Orangemen.

They swore he had ten thousand men all ready at his command,
All ready for to back the French as soon as they would land,
They swore he was committed to support the United cause,
The Judge he cried out: "Guilty", to be hanged by coercion laws.

One of those prosecutors, I often heard him tell,
It was at his father's table he was often treated well,
And in his brother's kitchen where many did he see,
The Byrnes were well rewarded for their civility.

My curse light on you Dixon, I ne'er will curse your soul,
It was at the Bench at Wicklow you swore without control,
The making of a false oath you thought it little sin,
To deprive the County Wicklow of the flower of all its men.

Where are you, Matthew Davis, or why don't you come on,
To prosecute the prisoner who now lies in Rathdrum?
The devil has him fast chained repenting for his sins,
In lakes of fire and brimstone and sulphur to the chin.

When the devil saw him coming he sang a merry song,
Saying, "Welcome Matthew Davis, what kept you out so long?
Where is that traitor, Dixon, to the Crown so loyal and true?
I have a warm corner for him and, of course, Bid Doolin, too."

Success to Billy Byrne! may his name forever shine,
Through Wicklow, Wexford and Kildare and all along the line,
May the Lord have mercy on his soul and all such souls as he,
Who stood upright for Ireland's cause and died for liberty.

THE CROPPY BOY
(A BALLAD OF '98)

William McBurney

The Wexford insurgents were known as "croppies" because, strongly influenced by the revolution in France, they cut their hair short Jacobin-fashion. In spite of some very approximate rhymes this plaintive song retains its power.

"Good men and true! in this house who dwell,
To a stranger bouchal I pray you tell,
Is the priest at home? or may he be seen?
I would speak a word with Father Green."
"The priest's at home, boy, and may be seen:
'Tis easy speaking with Father Green:
But you must wait till I go and see
If the holy father alone may be."

The youth has entered an empty hall—
What a lonely sound has his light foot-fall!
And the gloomy chamber's chill and bare,
With a vested priest in a lonely chair.
The youth has knelt to tell his sins,
"Nomine Dei", the youth begins
At "Mea culpa", he beats his breast,
And in broken murmurs he speaks the rest.

"At the siege of Ross did my father fall,
And at Gorey my loving brothers all;
I alone am left of my name and race,
I will go to Wexford and take their place,
I cursed three times since last Easter day—
At Mass-time once I went to play;
I passed the churchyard one day in haste
And forgot to pray for my mother's rest.

"I bear no hate against living thing,
But I love my country above my King,
Now, Father! bless me and let me go,
To die, if God has ordained it so."
The priest said naught, but a rustling noise
Made the youth look up in a wild surprise:
The robes were off, and in scarlet there
Sat a Yeoman captain with fiery glare.

With fiery glare and with fury hoarse,
Instead of a blessing he breathed a curse:—
"'Twas a good thought, boy, to come here and shrive,
For one short hour is your time to live.
Upon yon river three tenders float,
The priest's in one—if he isn't shot—
We hold this house for our lord and King,
And, Amen, say I, may all traitors swing!"

At Geneva Barracks that young man died.
And at Passage they have his body laid,
Good people, who live in peace and joy,
Breathe a prayer, shed a tear for the Croppy Boy.

The Croppy Boy

Anonymous

Another earlier version of the tale made more famous by Carroll Malone. "Lord Cornwall" is Cornwallis, the Lord-lieutenant. The tune was one of several used by Sean O'Riada in his incidental music for the film Mise Eire.

It was early, early in the spring,
When the small birds tune and the thrushes sing,
Changing their notes from tree to tree.
And the song they sung was Old Ireland free.

It was early, early on Tuesday night
When the yeomen cavalry gave me a fright,
To my misfortune and sad downfall
I was taken prisoner by Lord Cornwall.

It was to his guard-house I was led,
And in his parlour I was tried,
My sentence passed and my courage low
To new Geneva I was forced to go.

As I was going by my father's door
My brother William stood on the floor,
My aged father stood at the door,
And my tender mother her hair she tore.

As I was going through Wexford Street,
My own first cousin I there did meet,
My own first cousin did me betray,
And for one guinea swore my life away.

As I was going up Croppy Hill
Who could blame me if I cried my fill?
I looked behind and I looked before
My tender mother I could see no more.

My sister Mary heard the express
She ran downstairs in her morning dress,
One hundred guineas she would lay down
To see me liberated in Wexford town.

I choose the black and I choose the blue,
I forsook the red and orange too,
I did forsake them and did them deny,
And I'll wear the green like a Croppy Boy.

Farewell, father and mother, too,
And sister Mary, I have none but you,
And for my brother, he's all alone
He's pointing pikes on the grinding stone.

It was in Geneva this young man died
And in Geneva his body lies,
All good Christians now standing by
Pray the Lord have mercy on the Croppy Boy.

Bold Robert Emmet

Thomas Maguire

One of the most famous of all Irish ballads dedicated to Ireland's most popular insurgent. The author was an authentic street balladeer.

The struggle is over the boys are defeated,
Old Ireland's surrounded with sadness and gloom,
We were defeated and shamefully treated
And I, Robert Emmet awaiting my doom.
Hung, drawn and quartered, sure that was my sentence,
But soon I will show them no coward am I,
My crime is the love of the land I was born in,
A hero I lived and a hero I'll die.

Chorus
Bold Robert Emmet, the darling of Erin,
Bold Robert Emmet will die with a smile,
Farewell companions both loyal and daring,
I'll lay down my life for the Emerald Isle.

The barque lay at anchor awaiting to bring me
Over the billows to the land of the free;
But I must see my sweetheart for I know she will cheer me,
And with her I will sail far over the sea.
But I was arrested and cast into prison,
Tried as a traitor, a rebel, a spy;
But no one can call me a knave or a coward,
A hero I lived and a hero I'll die.

Chorus

Hark! the bell's tolling, I well know its meaning,
My poor heart tells me it is my death knell;
In come the clergy, the warder is leading,
I have no friends here to bid me farewell.
Good-bye, old Ireland, my parents and sweetheart,
Companions in arms to forget you must try;
I am proud of the honour, it was only my duty—
A hero I lived and a hero I'll die.

Chorus

A NEW SONG ON THE MANCHESTER MARTYRS
(OR THE SMASHING OF THE VAN)

Anonymous

A broadside account of the Bellvue Gaol rescue. The belief that the evidence against the men was unsafe did much to advance the Fenian cause.

Attend you gallant Irishmen and listen for a while
I'll sing to you the praises of the sons of Erin's Isle—
It's of those gallant heroes who voluntarily ran
To release two Irish Shamrocks, from an English prison van.
Hurrah my lads for freedom, let's all join heart and hand,
May the Lord have mercy on the boys that helped to smash the van.

On the eighteenth of September, it was a dreadful year,
When sorrow and excitement ran throughout all Lancashire,
At a gathering of the Irish boys they volunteered each man,
To release those Irish prisoners out of the prison van.

Kelly and Deasy were their names, I suppose you know them well,
Remanded for a week they were in Bellvue Gaol to dwell,
When taking of the prisoners back, their trial for to stand,
To make a safe deliverance they conveyed them in a van.

William Deasy was a man of good and noted fame,
Likewise Michael Larkin, we'll never forget his name,
With young Allen and O'Brien they took a part so grand,
In that glorious liberation and the smashing of the van.

In Manchester one morning those heroes did agree,
Their leaders, Kelly and Deasy, should have their liberty,
They drank a health to Ireland, and soon made up the plan,
To meet the prisoners on the road and take and smash the van.

With courage bold these heroes went and soon the van did stop,
They cleared the guards from back and front and then smashed in
    the top,
But in blowing open of the lock, they chanced to kill a man,
So three men must die on the scaffold high for smashing of the van.

One cold November morning in eighteen sixty-seven,
These martyrs to their country's cause a sacrifice were given,
"God save Ireland," was the cry, all through the crowd it ran,
The Lord have mercy on the boys that helped to smash the van.

So now kind friends I will conclude, I think it would be right,
That all true-hearted Irishmen together should unite,
Together should sympathise, my friends, and do the best we can
To keep the memories ever green, of the boys that smashed the van.

Down by the Glenside

Peadar Kearney

The best known of the ballads in praise of the Fenians, written by Brendan Behan's uncle who was also the author of the words of the Irish national anthem.

Down by the Glenside I met an old woman,
A plucking young nettles nor saw I was coming;
I listened awhile to the song she was hummin',
Glory O! Glory O! to the Bold Fenian Men.

"'Tis fifty long years since I saw the moon beamin'
On strong manly forms, an' on eyes with hope gleamin'
I see them again sure thro' all my day-dreamin':
Glory O! Glory O! to the Bold Fenian Men.

"When I was a girl their marchin' an' drillin'
Awoke in the glenside sound awesome an' thrillin',
They loved poor old Ireland an' to die they were willin';
Glory O! Glory O! to the Bold Fenian Men.

"Some died by the glenside, some died 'mid the stranger,
And wise men have told us their cause was a failure,
But they stood by old Ireland an' never feared danger,
Glory O! Glory O! to the Bold Fenian Men."

I passed on my way, God be praised that I met her,
Be life long or short I shall never forget her,
We may have great men, but we'll never have better,
Glory O! Glory O! to the Bold Fenian Men.

The Foggy Dew

Anonymous

Ballad of 1916 written while the memory of the battles of Suvla Bay (Gallipoli) and Sud-el-Bar (Mesopotamia) were still fresh. The word "sons" in the second last line of the second verse replaces the contemporary "huns."

As down the glen, one Easter morn,
To a City fair rode I,
There armed lines of marching men,
In squadrons passed me by;
No pipes did hum nor battle drum
Did sound its dread tattoo,
But the Angelus bell o'er the Liffey swell
Rang out in the Foggy Dew.

Right proudly high over Dublin town,
They hung out the flag of war,
'Twas better to die 'neath an Irish sky
Than at Suvla or Sudelbar;
And from the plains of royal Meath
Strong men came hurrying through
While Britannia's sons with their great guns
Sailed in by the Foggy Dew.

The night fell black but the rifles' crack
Made perfidious Albion reel
'Mid leaden rain seven tongues of flame
Did burn o'er the lines of steel.
By each shining blade a prayer was said
That to Ireland her sons might be true
And when morning broke still the war flag shook
Its folds in the Foggy Dew.

But the bravest fell and the sullen bell
Rang mournfully and clear
For those who died that Easter tide
In the springing of the year.
And the world did gaze with deep amaze
On those fearless men but few,
Who bore the fight that freedom's light,
Might shine thro' the Foggy Dew.

'Twas England bade our wild geese go
That small nations might be free
But their lonely graves are by Suvla's waves
And the fringe of the grey North sea.
O! had they died by Pearse's side
Or fought with Valera too
Their place we'd keep where the Fenians sleep
'Neath the hills of the Foggy Dew.

Back to the glen I rode again,
And my heart with grief was sore,
For I parted then with valiant men
I never would see more;
But to and fro in my dreams I go,
And I kneel and pray for you,
For slavery fled, O! rebel dead
When you fell in the Foggy Dew.

KEVIN BARRY

Anonymous

Famous War of Independence street ballad about the eighteen-year-old medical student who was hanged for his part in a raid in Church Street, Dublin in which six soldiers were killed. The song became so popular with the British soldiers that it was banned.

In Mountjoy jail one Monday morning,
High upon the gallows tree
Kevin Barry gave his young life,
For the cause of liberty,
But a lad of eighteen summers,
Yet no one can deny,
As he walked to death that morning,
He proudly held his head on high.

Just before he faced the hangman,
In his dreary prison cell,
British soldiers tortured Barry,
Just because he would not tell
The names of his brave companions,
And other things they wished to know,
"Turn informer or we'll kill you,"
Kevin Barry answered "No."

Calmly standing to "attention,"
While he bade his last farewell
To his broken-hearted mother,
Whose grief no one can tell.
For the cause he proudly cherished,
This sad parting had to be;
Then to death walked softly smiling,
That old Ireland might be free.

Another martyr for old Ireland,
Another murder for the crown,
Whose brutal laws may kill the Irish,
But can't keep their spirit down.
Lads like Barry are no cowards,
From the foe they will not fly,
Lads like Barry will free Ireland,
For her sake they'll live and die.

A Squeeze of Orange

LILLIBULÉRO

Anonymous

The tune that "whistled James II out of three kingdoms" written in response to the appointment of Richard Talbot, Earl of Tyrconnel as Lord Deputy by Thomas, 1st Marquis of Wharton. The refrain is a mocking parody of the Catholic watch-cry during their rising in 1641, An lile ba léir é; ba linne an lá (The lily prevailed; the day was ours.)

Ho brother Teig, dost hear the decree
Lillibuléro bullen a la
Dat we shall have a new Debittie
Lillibuléro bullen a la.
Chorus
Léro léro léro léro
Lillibuléro bulena la
Lillibuléro léro léro
Lillibuléro bullen a la.

Ho, by my Soul, it is a Talbot;
Lillibuléro, etc.
And he will cut all de English throat,
Lillibuléro, etc.

Though, by my Soul, de English do prate,
Lillibuléro, etc.
De Law's on dere side and de divil knows what
Lillibuléro, etc.

But if Dispence do come from the Pope,
Lillibuléro, etc.
We'll hang Magna Cart and demselves in a rope,
Lillibuléro, etc.

And the good Talbot is now made a Lord,
Lillibuléro, etc.
And with his brave lads he's coming aboard,
Lillibuléro, etc.

Who all in France have taken a swear,
Lillibuléro, etc.
Dat day will have no Protestant heir,
Lillibuléro, etc.

O but why does he stay behind?
Lillibuléro, etc.
Ho, by my Soul, 'tis a Protestant wind,
Lillibuléro, etc.

Now that Tyrconnel is come ashore,
Lillibuléro, etc.
And we shall have Commissions *go leór*,
Lillibuléro, etc.

And he dat will not go to the Mass,
Lillibuléro, etc.
Shall be turned out and look like an ass,
Lillibuléro, etc.

Now, now de hereticks all will go down,
Lillibuléro, etc.
By Christ and St. Patrick the nation's our own.
Lillibuléro, etc.

Dere was an old prophecy found in a bog,
Lillibuléro, etc.
Dat our land would be ruled by an ass and a dog.
Lillibuléro, etc.

So now dis old Prophecy's coming to pass,
Lillibuléro, etc.
For James is de dog and Tyrconnel's de ass.
Lillibuléro, etc.

No Surrender

Charlotte Elizabeth Tonna

Song of the resistance of the Derry apprentices who on 7 December 1688 shut the gates of the city against the Catholic regiment of Lord Antrim. On 18 April 1689 James II himself was refused admission and the siege of the city began. It was lifted on 31 July when the Mountjoy *broke the boom that had been placed across the river Foyle.*

Behold the crimson banners float,
O'er yonder turrets hoary,
They tell of deeds of mighty note,
And Derry's dauntless glory;
When her brave sons undaunted stood
Embattled to defend her
Indignant stemmed oppression's flood,
And sung out "No Surrender."

Old Derry's walls were firm and strong,
Well fenced in every quarter—
Each frowning bastion, grim along,
With culverin and mortar:
But Derry had a surer guard
Than all that art would lend her
Her 'prentice hearts the gates who barred,
And sung out "No Surrender!"

On came the foe in bright attire,
And fierce the assault was given;
By shot and shell, 'mid streams of fire,
Her fated roofs were riven.
But baffled was the tyrant's wrath,
And vain his hopes to bend her,
For still, 'mid famine, fire and death,
She sung out "No Surrender!"

Again when treasons maddened round,
And rebel hordes were swarming
Were Derry's sons the foremost found
For King and Country arming;
Forth, forth, they rush at Honour's call
From age to boyhood tender,
Again to man their virgin wall
And sing out "No Surrender!"

Long may the crimson banner wave,
A meteor streaming airy,
Portentous of the free and brave,
Who man the walls of Derry.
And Derry's sons alike defy
Pope, Traitor, or Pretender;
And peal to Heaven their 'prentice cry
Their patriot—"No Surrender!"

THE BOYNE WATER

Anonymous

*Orange ballad in celebration of the famous but indecisive battle of 1 July
1690 which revealed that James II was no general.*

July the First, of a morning clear, one thousand six hundred and
    ninety,
King William did his men prepare—of thousands he had thirty—
To fight King James and all his foes, encamped near the Boyne
    Water;
He little feared, though two to one, their multitude to scatter.

King William called his officers, saying "Gentlemen, mind your
    station,
And let your valour here be shown before this Irish nation;
My brazen walls let no man break, and your subtle foes you'll
    scatter,
Be sure you show them good English play as you go over the
    water."

Both foot and horse they marched on, intending them to batter,
But the brave Duke Schomberg he was shot as he crossed over the
    water.
When that King William did observe the brave Duke Schomberg
    falling,
He reined his horse with a heavy heart, on the Enniskilleners
    calling:

"What will you do for me, brave boys—see yonder men retreating?
Our enemies encouraged are, and English drums are beating."
He says, "My boys feel no dismay at the losing of one commander,
For God shall be our King this day, and I'll be general under."

Within four yards of our fore-front, before a shot was fired,
A sudden snuff they got that day, which little they desired;
For horse and man fell to the ground, and some hung in their saddle:
Others turned up their forked ends, which we call *coup de ladle*.

Prince Eugene's regiment was the next, on our right hand advanced
Into a field of standing wheat, where Irish horses pranced;
But the brandy ran so in their heads, their senses all did scatter,
They little thought to leave their bones that day at the Boyne Water.

Both men and horse lay on the ground, and many there lay bleeding,
I saw no sickles there that day—but, sure, there was sharp shearing.
Now, praise God, all true Protestants, and heaven's and earth's
    Creator,
For the deliverance he sent our enemies to scatter.
The Church's foes will pine away, like churlish hearted Nabal.
For our deliverer came this day like the great Zorobabel.

So praise God, all true Protestants, and I will say no further,
But had the Papists gained the day, there would have been open
    murder.
Although King James and many more were ne'er that way inclined,
It was not in their power to stop what the rabble they designed.

CROPPIES LIE DOWN

Anonymous

The Orange answer to the risings of 1798. The order was formed after the famous "battle of the Diamond" near Loughgall in September 1795. It is interesting that the Orangemen called themselves "soldiers of Erin."

We soldiers of Erin, so proud of the name,
Will rise upon Rebels and Frenchmen our fame;
We'll fight to the last in the honest old cause,
And guard our religion, our freedom, and laws;
We'll fight for our country, our king, and his crown,
And make all the traitors and croppies lie down.

Down, down, croppies lie down.

The rebels so bold—when they've none to oppose—
To houses and hay-stacks are terrible foes;
They murder poor parsons, and also their wives,
But soldiers at once make them run for their lives;
And wherever we march, thro' the country or town,
In ditches or cellars, the croppies lie down.

United in blood, to their country's disgrace,
They secretly shoot whom they dare not to face;
But when we can catch the sly rogues in the field,
A handful of soldiers make hundreds to yield,
And the cowards collect but to raise our renown,
For as soon as we fire the croppies lie down.

While they, in the war that unmanly they wage
On woman herself turn their blood-thirsty rage,
We'll fly to protect the dear creatures from harms,
And shelter them safely when clasp'd in our arms:
On love in a soldier no maiden will frown,
But bless the dear boys that made croppies lie down.

Should France e'er attempt, or by fraud or by guile,
Her forces to land on our emerald isle,
We'll shew that they ne'er can make free soldiers slaves,
And only possess our green fields for their graves;
Our country's applauses our triumph will crown,
While low with the French, brother, croppies lie down.

When wars and when dangers again shall be o'er,
And peace with her blessings revisit our shore;
When arms we relinquish, no longer to roam,
With pride will our families welcome us home,
And drink, as in bumpers past troubles we drown,
A health to the lads that made croppies lie down.

DOLLY'S BRAE

Anonymous

Part of the Orange martyrology describing the encounter of Ribbonmen and Orangemen near Castlewellan, Co. Down, on 12 July 1849.

On the twelfth of July in the year forty-nine,
Some rebels together thought fit to combine,
Our few orange heroes to murder and slay,
They assembled in thousands around Dolly's Brae.
Derry down, down, down, derry down.

For years have some statesmen conceded to those,
Who at heart are dark papists and Britain's false foes,
Their impudence risen—they dared then to say,
That our Orangemen should not pass o'er Dolly's Brae.

From March, Forty-nine, they had plotted and schemed,
As they'd oft done before, for the traitors had deemed
That as at Crossgar they would murder and slay,
And slaughter our Orangemen at Dolly's Brae.

M'Dowell, your innocent blood rose on high,
And the God of your fathers regarded your cry,
The treacherous dogs who killed you on that day,
On the twelfth were defeated at famed Dolly's Brae.

But "vengeance is mine," and our God still is true,
He has often supported the Orange and Blue.
Enniskillen and Aughrim, Boyne and Derry can say,
That our forefathers conquered as at Dolly's Brae.

No more shall those rebels attempt to subdue
Our veterans of loyal true Orange and Blue,
No more dare to stop us, or point out the way.
That we'll march, colours flying, o'er famed Dolly's Brae.

Then here's great success to true Orangemen's cause,
Our Queen, gallant Roden, and Protestant laws,
And let famed Dolly's Brae, where our foes got their fill,
Be remembered for ever as King William's Hill.

THE ORANGE LILY-O

Anonymous

Innocent flower, Lilium bulbiferum, *which has become a political symbol. The song in a rougher version may be heard in July throughout the marching season.*

Oh did you go to see the show,
Each rose and pink a-dilly-o,
To feast your eyes upon the prize,
Won by the Orange Lily-o.

The Viceroy there so debonair,
Just like a daffydilly-o,
And Lady Clarke, blithe as a lark,
Approached the Orange Lily-o.

Then heigh-o the Lily-o,
The royal loyal Lily-o.
Beneath the sky what flow'r can vie,
With Ireland's Orange Lily-o.

The elated muse, to hear the news,
Jumped like a Connacht filly-o,
As gossip fame did loud proclaim
The triumph of the Lily-o;

The lowland field may roses yield,
Gay heaths the highlands hilly-o,
But high or low, no flower can show,
Like the glorious Orange Lily-o.

Then heigho the lily-o,
The royal, loyal lily-o,
There's not a flower in Erin's bower
Can match the Orange Lily-o.

The Lighter Side

BRIAN O LINN

Anonymous

*Late eighteenth-century ballad but based on a much older Scots
nursery rhyme "Tam O'Linn." The intention was as ever to insult the
non-English. The last verse is usually included in* Mother Goose.

Brian O Linn had no breeches to wear
He got an old sheepskin to make him a pair
With the fleshy side out and the woolly side in,
"They'll be pleasant and cool," says Brian O Linn.

Brian O Linn had no shirt to his back,
He went to a neighbour's, and borrowed a sack,
Then he puckered the meal bag in under his chin—
"Sure they'll take them for ruffles," says Brian O Linn.

Brian O Linn was hard up for a coat,
So he borrowed the skin of a neighbouring goat,
With the horns sticking out from his oxsters, and then,
"Sure they'll take them for pistols," says Brian O Linn.

Brian O Linn had no hat to put on,
So he got an old beaver to make him a one,
There was none of the crown left and less of the brim,
"Sure there's fine ventilation," says Brian O Linn.

Brian O Linn had no brogues for his toes,
He hopped in two crab-shells to serve him for those.
Then he split up two oysters that match'd like a twin,
"Sure they'll shine out like buckles," says Brian O Linn.

Brian O Linn had no watch to put on,
So he scooped out a turnip to make him a one.
Then he placed a young cricket in under the skin—
"Sure they'll think it is ticking," says Brian O Linn.

Brian O Linn to his house had no door,
He'd the sky for a roof, and the bog for a floor;
He'd a way to jump out, and a way to swim in,
"'Tis a fine habitation," says Brian O Linn.

Brian O Linn went a-courting one night,
He set both the mother and daughter to fight;
To fight for his hand they both stripped to the skin,
"Sure! I'll marry you both," says Brian O Linn.

Brian O Linn, his wife and wife's mother,
They all lay down in the bed together,
The sheets they were old and the blankets were thin,
"Lie close to the wall," says Brian O Linn.

Brian O Linn, his wife and wife's mother,
Were all going home o'er the bridge together,
The bridge it broke down, and they all tumbled in,
"We'll go home by the water," says Brian O Linn.

Johnny, I Hardly Knew Ye

Anonymous

*Blackly comic ballad dating from the early nineteenth century when
Irish soldiers were used by the East India Company to quell a rising
in Ceylon.*

While going the road to sweet Athy,
Hurroo! hurroo!
While going the road to sweet Athy,
Hurroo! hurroo!
While going the road to sweet Athy,
A stick in my hand and a drop in my eye,
A doleful damsel I heard cry:
"Och, Johnny, I hardly knew ye!
With drums and guns, and guns and drums
The enemy nearly slew ye;
My darling dear, you look so queer,
Och, Johnny, I hardly knew ye!

"Where are your eyes that looked so mild?
Hurroo! hurroo!
Where are your eyes that looked so mild?
Hurroo! hurroo!
Where are your eyes that looked so mild,
When my poor heart you first beguiled?
Why did you run from me and the child?
Och, Johnny, I hardly knew ye!
With drums, etc.

"Where are the legs with which you run?
Hurroo! hurroo!
Where are the legs with which you run?
Hurroo! hurroo!
Where are the legs with which you run
When you went to carry a gun?
Indeed, your dancing days are done!
Och, Johnny, I hardly knew ye!
With drums etc.

"It grieved my heart to see you sail,
Hurroo! hurroo!
It grieved my heart to see you sail,
Hurroo! hurroo!
It grieved my heart to see you sail,
Though from my heart you took leg-bail;
Like a cod you're doubled up head and tail.
Och, Johnny, I hardly knew ye!
With drums etc.

"You haven't an arm and you haven't a leg,
Hurroo! hurroo!
You haven't an arm and you haven't a leg,
Hurroo! hurroo!
You haven't an arm and you haven't a leg,
You're an eyeless, noseless, chickenless egg;
You'll have to be put with a bowl to beg:
Och, Johnny, I hardly knew ye!
With drums etc.

"I'm happy for to see you home,
Hurroo! hurroo!
I'm happy for to see you home,
Hurroo! hurroo!
I'm happy for to see you home,
All from the island of Sulloon,
So low in flesh, so high in bone;
Och, Johnny, I hardly knew ye!
With drums etc.

"But sad as it is to see you so,
Hurroo! hurroo!
But sad as it is to see you so,
Hurroo! hurroo!
But sad as it is to see you so,
And to think of you now as an object of woe,
Your Peggy'll still keep ye on as her beau;
Och, Johnny, I hardly knew ye!
With drums and guns, and guns and drums
The enemy nearly slew ye;
My darling dear, you look so queer,
Och, Johnny, I hardly knew ye!"

DICEY REILLY

Anonymous

Lines in celebration of a Dublin alcoholic. The "pop" is, of course, a pawnbroker's shop.

Ah poor oul Dicey Reilly, she has taken to the sup,
And poor oul Dicey Reilly she will never give it up,
It's off each morning to the pop that she goes in for another little
    drop,
But the heart of the rowl is Dicey Reilly.

She will walk along Fitzgibbon Street with an independent air
And then it's down by Summerhill, and as the people stare
She'll say "It's nearly half past one, time I went in for another
    little one."
But the heart of the rowl is Dicey Reilly.

Now at two, pubs close and out she goes as happy as a lark
She'll find a bench to sleep it off down in St Patrick's Park.
She'll wake at five feeling in the pink and say "Tis time for
    another drink."
But the heart of the rowl is Dicey Reilly.

Now she'll travel far to a dockside bar to have another round
And after one or two or three she doesn't feel quite sound
And after four she's a bit unstable, after five underneath the table
The heart of the rowl is Dicey Reilly.

Oh they carry her home at twelve o'clock as they do every night
Bring her inside, put her on the bed and then turn out the light.
Next morning she'll get out of bed and look for a curer for her
head
But the heart of the rowl is Dicey Reilly.

Ah poor oul Dicey Reilly she has taken to the sup
And poor oul Dicey Reilly she will never give it up.
It's off each morning to the pop then she goes in for another little
drop
But the heart of the rowl is Dicey Reilly.

THE MULLINGAR HEIFER

Anonymous

Comic song which takes its title and its fame from the last line of the antepenultimate verse. It was and is very popular and has the capacity for extra stanzas to be added ad lib *by local bards.*

In Dublin's fair city where fine people dwell
Their fortunes would take me too long for to tell
There's one millionaire in the city 'tis true
But he isn't Irish, he is only a Jew.

The people of Limerick have got a fine name
Their hams and their bacons are well known to fame
Their sausages too are the finest of meat
While the people of Dublin eat only pig's feet.

Old Maguire of Clonmel was that fond of his bed
His poor wife he nearly drove off of her head
At last for the villain she did prove a match
For she gave him twelve duck eggs and told him to hatch.

The Kilkenny lads are fine rovin' blades
And make a good match for the Kilkenny maids
And when they get married they all wear silk hats
To rear up the kittens of the Kilkenny cats.

A Belfast girl said 'a blonde I'd like to be'
So she bought a bottle at a swell pharmacy,
Something exploded her peroxide
She thought she was dead but she was only dyed.

When a Galway girl got married in days long dead
She got for her fortune a fine feather bed,
When a girl now gets married they think it enough
To give her a lipstick and a new powder puff.

There was an elopement down in Mullingar
But sad to relate the pair didn't get far
"Oh fly" said he, "Darling and see how it feels"
But the Mullingar heifer was beef to the heels.

A barber in Trim used get gay with the girls
Who came to his parlour to shingle their curls
His wife caught him giving a permanent wave
Now the poor fellow lies in a permanent grave.

A Cork lad who stammered was once getting wed
And he practiced beforehand the words to be said
"Will you take this woman" the parson did press
And he had to say "no" because he couldn't say "yes...es."

The Agricultural Girl or Mary Ann Malone

Anonymous

A rather tongue-in-cheek paean for something genuinely Irish. The reference to Ouida—the pen-name of Louise de la Ramée (1839-1908)—author of the famous romance of the French Foreign Legion, Under Two Flags (1867), *dates it as late nineteenth-century.*

If all the women in the town were bundled together,
The girl I love would beat them all in every kind of weather
The rain can't wash her powder off because she does not
    wear it
Her face and figure's all her own - that's true for I declare it

chorus
For she's a great big stout strong lump of an agricultural
    Irish girl,
She never paints nor powders and her figure's all her own
For she can strike so hard you would think you were hit by
    the kick of a mule
The full of the house of Irish love, is Mary Ann Malone.

She's no grand education she's only just past her letters
But for anything like a lady I should like to find her betters
She does not read Ouida's works, or Bow-Bella fashion pages
And she does not wear those things behind the ladies call
    bird-cages.

She was only seventeen last grass, and still improving greatly,
I wonder what she'll be like when her bones have set completely
You'd think your hand was in a vice, whenever she shakes it,
And if there's any cash about it's Mary Ann who takes it.

Coortin' In the Kitchen

Anonymous

Comic Dublin ballad dating from the 1830s. There is a more modern version with all the historical piquancy bled out of it. The "Repealer's coat" was a greatcoat with a badge showing that the wearer was a supporter of Daniel O'Connell, then in his prime as "King of the Beggars."

Come single belle and beau to me now pay attention,
And love I'll plainly show is the divil's own invention,
For once in love I fell with a maiden's smiles bewitching,
Miss Henrietta Bell down in Captain Phibbs's kitchen.

Chorus
Ritooralooral lah
Ritooralooral addy
Ritooralooral lah
Ritooralooral addy.

At the age of seventeen I was tied unto a grocer,
Not far from Stephen's Green, where Miss Bell for tea would
    go, sir.
Her manners were so free, she set my heart a-twitching,
She invited me to tea, down in Captain Phibbs's kitchen.

Next Sunday being the day, we were to have the flare-up,
I dressed myself quite gay, an' I frizz'd and oiled my hair up.
As the captain had no wife, he had gone out a fishin',
So we kicked up high life, below-stairs in the kitchen.

Just as the clock struck six we sat down to the table;
She handed tea and cakes—I ate while I was able.
I ate cakes, drank punch and tea, till my side had got a stitch in,
And the hours flew quick away, while coortin' in the kitchen.

With my arms round her waist I kissed—she hinted marriage—
To the door in dreadful haste came Captain Phibbs's carriage.
Her looks told me full well, that moment she was wishin'
That I'd get out to H——, or somewhere far from the kitchen.

She flew up off my knees, full five feet up or higher,
And over head and heels, threw me slap into the fire.
My new Repealer's coat, that I bought from Mr. Stitchen
With a thirty-shilling note, went to blazes in the kitchen.

I grieved to see my duds, all besmeared with smoke and ashes,
When a tub of dirty suds, right in my face she dashes,
As I lay on the floor still the water she kept pitchin',
Till the footman broke the door, and marched down into the
    kitchen.

When the captain came down stairs, though he seen my
    situation,
In spite of all my prayers I was marched off to the station.
For me they'd take no bail, tho' to get home I was itchin',
But I had to tell the tale, of how I came into the kitchen.

I said she did invite me, but she gave a flat denial,
For assault she did indict me, and I was sent for trial.
She swore I robbed the house in spite of all her screechin'.
So I six months went round the rack for courtin' in the kitchen.

The Strabane Fleet

Anonymous

Gripping account of an epic voyage of fourteen miles along the savage headwaters of the Foyle. The reference to the New-bridge dates it as sometime after 1863.

Come all you jolly seamen bold
That plough the raging main,
Give an ear unto my tragedy
And I'll relate the same.
Our Shamrock slowly moved off,
And I in her did go;
That very night at six o'clock,
The stormy winds did blow.

Her steaming works remained untouched
For two long hours or more,
She logged and heaved most dangerously,
Not very far from shore.
Her cabin windows were all broke,
There scarcely were left one,
When the Mate cries to the Captain,
"Sir, we'll never reach Strabane."

When we came to the New-bridge,
No danger did we fear;
Our Captain he stood on the deck
And told me for to steer.
"Oh, it's steer your helm and port, my boy,
With your bow's towards the lan',
For I think we'll have rough weather
Before we reach Strabane."

The raging seas rolled mountains high,
No mercy from the wave;
We expected every minute
That we'd find a watery grave.
The second shock the Shamrock got
All hands were bound to cry:
"May the Lord have mercy on our souls,
For near Prehen we lie."

We took our way to Carrigans,
No danger did we fear,
But looking towards St. Johnston
No light-house did appear.
The raging seas rolled mountains high
And the wind was blowing strong.
When the Mate cries to the Captain:
"Sir, Oh, yonder's Dunalong!"

Oh! it's Dunalong, that seaport town,
If we were landed there,
We would have the best of harbour,
And no danger might we fear.
We'll steer our course for Dunalong,
For I think it's our best plan,
Or else the Shamrock might be lost—
The fleet bound for Strabane.

The wind it changed to the North-West,
And dreadful was the night,
We looked out towards Porthall,
But we could see no light.
It's "count your men," the Captain cried,
"For I think we've lost M'Shane."
It was a dreadful passage
In the fleet bound for Strabane!

The crew being hearty all the way,
They sang an old sea song;
"O, Molly, I love your daughter—
I love no other one."
The wind it changed to the North-East,
And then came on a squall:
All the grub we had on board
Was a bottle of castor oil.

Thank God we landed in Strabane,
No danger do we fear;
We'll drink a health to seamen bold
And brave, while we lie here.
When looking over Derry Bridge
There is nothing half so gran'
As to view the fleet that sails the deep,
From Derry to Strabane.

THE OLD LEATHER BREECHES

Anonymous

Indigestible song famous before the days of the Good Food Guide. A "burgoo" was a sailor's dish of oatmeal boiled with salt, sugar and butter.

At the Sign of the Bell on the road to Clonmel
Paddy Hegarty kept a neat shebeen,
He sold pig's meat and bread, kept a fine lodging bed
And was liked in the country he lived in.
Himself and his wife, both struggled through life
On weekdays Pat mended the ditches
But on Sundays he dressed in a suit of the best
And his pride was his old leather breeches.

For twenty-one years at least so it appears,
His father these breeches had run in,
And the morning he died, he to his bedside
Called Paddy, his own darling son, in;
His advice then he gave ere he went to his grave!
And he bade him take care of his riches,
Says he, "It's no use to step into my shoes,
But I'd like you'd leap into my breeches."

Now last winter's snow left victuals so low
That Paddy was ate out completely,
With the snow coming down he could not get to town
Thoughts of hunger did bother him greatly
One night as he lay adreaming away
Of ghosts, fairies, spirits and witches,
He heard an uproar, just outside his door,
And he jumped up to pull on his breeches.

— 68 —

Says Brian McGurk, with a voice like a Turk,
Come, Paddy, and get us some eating,
Says Big Andy Moore, we'll burst open the door,
Sure this is no night to be waiting;
The words were scarce spoke when the door it was broke,
And they crowded round Paddy like leeches,
And they swore by the hob, if they didn't get prog,
They would eat him clean out of his breeches.

Poor Paddy in dread slipped up to his bed
That held Judy his own darling wife in;
And there 'twas agreed that they should get a feed,
So he slipped out and brought a big knife in;
He cut out the waist of his breeches, the beast,
And he ripped out the buttons and stitches,
And he cut them in stripes, the way they do tripes,
And he boiled them his old leather breeches.

The tripes they were stewed, on a dish they were strewed,
And the boys all roared out: Lord be thankit,
But Hegarty's wife was afraid of her life
And she thought it high time for to shank it;
To see how they smiled for they thought Paddy boiled
Some mutton or beef of the richest,
But little they knew it was leather burgoo
That was made out of Paddy's ould breeches.

As they messed on the stuff says Darby, it's tough,
Says Andy "you're no judge of mutton,"
When Brian McGurk, on the point of his fork,
Held up a big ivory button;
Says Paddy, what's that, sure I thought it was fat,
Brian leps to his feet and he screeches:
"Be the powers above, I was trying to shove
Me teeth through the flap of his breeches."

They all flew at Pat, but he cut out of that,
He ran when he saw them all rising;
Says Brian, make haste, and go for the priest,
Be the holy Saint Patrick, I'm poisoned;
Revenge for the joke they had, for they broke
All the chairs, bowls, and tables, and dishes,
And from that very night they'd broke out your daylight
If they'd catch you with old leather breeches.

Mrs McGrath

Anonymous

Ribald anti-recruiting song that was adopted in an ironic way by the Irish Volunteers in 1913 but it certainly dates back to at least Napoleonic times.

"Oh Mrs. McGrath!" the sergeant said,
"Would you like to make a soldier out of your son, Ted,
With a scarlet coat and a big cocked hat,
Now Mrs. McGrath, wouldn't you like that?"

Chorus
Wid yer too-ri-aa, fol-the-diddle-aa,
Too-ri-oo-ri-oo-ri-aa,
Wid yer too-ri-aa fol-the-diddle-aa
Too-ri-oo-ri-oo-ri-aa.
Lav beg, the Cracker, O.

So Mrs. McGrath lived on the sea-shore
For the space of seven long years or more
Till she saw a big ship sailing into the bay
"Here's my son Ted, wisha, clear the way."
Chorus

"Oh, Captain dear, where have you been
Have you been sailing on the Mediterreen
Or have ye any tidings of my son Ted
Is the poor boy living or is he dead?"
Chorus

Then up comes Ted without any legs
And in their place he has two wooden pegs
She kissed him a dozen times or two
Saying, "Holy Moses 'tisn't you."
Chorus

"Oh then were ye drunk or were ye blind
That ye left yer two fine legs behind
Or was it walking upon the sea
Wore yer two fine legs from the knees away?"
Chorus

"Oh I wasn't drunk and I wasn't blind
But I left my two fine legs behind
For a cannon ball on the fifth of May
Took my two fine legs from the knees away."
Chorus

"Oh then Teddy me boy," the widow cried,
"Yer two fine legs were yer mammy's pride
Them stumps of a tree wouldn't do at all
Why didn't ye run from the big cannon ball?
Chorus

All foreign wars I do proclaim
Between Don John and the King of Spain
And by herrins I'll make them rue the time
That they swept the legs from a child of mine.
Chorus

Oh then, if I had you back again
I'd never let ye go to fight the King of Spain
For I'd rather my Ted as he used to be
Than the King of France and his whole Navee."
Chorus

WHACK FOL THE DIDDLE

Peadar Kearney

Comic song current at the time of the reactivation of the Irish Republican Brotherhood in 1914. Béal an Átha Buidhe refers to the battle of the Yellow Ford (14 August 1598) when Hugh O'Neill defeated the English forces and killed their captain Sir Henry Bagenal. Pieter's Hill was a skirmish in which soldiers of the Irish brigade fighting on the side of the Boers helped defeat the Crown forces in 1899.

I sing you a song of peace and love,
Whack fol the diddle lol the di do day.
To the land that reigns all lands above,
Whack fol the diddle lol the di do day.
May peace and plenty be her share,
Who kept our homes from want and care,
Oh God bless England is our prayer,
Whack fol the diddle lol the di do day.

Chorus
Whack fol the diddle lol the di do day.
So we say Hip Hurrah!
Come and listen while we pray
Whack fol the diddle lol the di do day.

When we were savage, fierce and wild,
Whack fol the diddle lol the di do day.
She came as a mother to her child,
Whack fol the diddle lol the di do day.
Gently raised us from the slime,
Kept our hands from hellish crime,
And sent us to heaven in her own good time,
Whack fol the diddle lol the di do day.
Chorus

Our fathers oft' were naughty boys,
Whack fol the diddle lol the di do day.
Pikes and guns are dangerous toys,
Whack fol the diddle lol the di do day.
From Béal an Átha Buidhe to Pieters Hill
They made poor England weep her fill,
But old Britannia loves us still,
Whack fol the diddle lol the di do day.
Chorus

Oh Irishmen forget the past,
Whack fol the diddle lol the di do day.
And think of the day that is coming fast,
Whack fol the diddle lol the di do day.
When we shall all be civilised
Neat and clean and well advised,
Oh won't Mother England be surprised!
Whack fol the diddle lol the di do day.
Chorus

The Oul' Man From Killyburn Brae

Anonymous

Ulster sexist tract sometimes known as "The Women Are Worse than the Men."

Is it true that the women are worse than the men?
Right fol, right fol, tiddy fol-ay.
Is it true that the women are worse
than the men?
That they went down to Hell and were threw out again?
With your right fol lol, tiddy fol lol,
Fol the dol lol the dol lol the dol day.

There was an oul' man of Killyburn Brae,
Right fol, right fol, tiddy fol-ay.
There was an oul' man of Killyburn Brae,
Had a scoldin' oul' wife for the most of his day
With your right fol lol, tiddy fol lol,
Fol the dol lol the dol lol the dol day.

One day as this man he walked out in the Glen,
Right fol, right fol, tiddy fol-ay.
One day as this man he walked out in the Glen
He met with the devil sayin' "How are you then?"
With your right fol lol, tiddy fol lol,
Fol the dol lol the dol lol the dol day.

Sez he "Me oul' man I have come for your wife,"
Right fol, right fol, tiddy fol-ay.
Sez he, "Me oul' man I have come for your wife
For I hear she's the plague and torment of your life"
With your right fol lol, tiddy fol lol,
Fol the dol lol the dol lol the dol day.

So the Divil he hoisted her up on his back,
Right fol, right fol, tiddy fol-ay.
So the Divil he hoisted her up on his back
And he hustled for Hell with her tied in a sack,
With your right fol lol, tiddy fol lol,
Fol the dol lol the dol lol the dol day.

And when at the finish they got to Hell's gate,
Right fol, right fol, tiddy fol-ay.
And when at the finish they got to Hell's gate
He threw her right down with a bump on her pate
With your right fol lol, tiddy fol lol,
Fol the dol lol the dol lol the dol day.

There were two little divils there tied up with chains,
Right fol, right fol, tiddy fol-ay.
There were two little divils there tied up with chains
She up with her stick and she scattered their brains
With your right fol lol, tiddy fol lol,
Fol the dol lol the dol lol the dol day.

There were four little divils a-playin' hand-ball,
Right fol, right fol, tiddy fol-ay.
There were four little divils a-playin' hand-ball
She up with her stick an' she scattered them all
With your right fol lol, tiddy fol lol,
Fol the dol lol the dol lol the dol day.

So the divil he hoisted her up on his back,
Right fol, right fol, tiddy fol-ay.
So the divil he hoisted her up on his back,
They were seven years goin', nine days coming back
With your right fol lol, tiddy fol lol,
Fol the dol lol the dol lol the dol day.

Sez he, "Me oul' man here's your wife, safe and well,"
Right fol, right fol, tiddy fol-ay.
Sez he, "Me oul' man here's your wife, safe and well
For the likes of herself we would not have in Hell."
With your right fol lol, tiddy fol lol,
Fol the dol lol the dol lol the dol day.

So it's true that the women are worse than the men,
Right fol, right fol, tiddy fol-ay.
So it's true that the women are worse than the men,
When they go down to Hell they are threw out again.
With your right fol lol, tiddy fol lol,
Fol the dol lol the dol lol the dol day.

THE COD LIVER OIL

Anonymous

A cure-all, most efficacious in every case, that ante-dated Lily the Pink's by sixty years.

I'm a young married man
And I'm tired of my life,
For lately I married,
An ailing young wife,
She does nothing all day,
Only sit down and sigh,
Saying I wish to the Lord,
That I only could die.

Till a friend of my own,
Came to see me one day,
And told me my wife
Was just pining away,
But he afterwards told me
That she would get strong
If I'd buy her a bottle
From Doctor de Jongh.

So I bought her a bottle
'Twas just for a try,
And the way that she scoffed it,
You'd swear she was dry;
I bought her another,
It went just the same,
Till I own she's got
Cod Liver Oil on the brain.

My house it resembles
A big doctor's shop
With bottles and bottles
From bottom to top
And when in the morning
The kettle's a-boil
Ye'd swear it was singing out
"Cod Liver Oil!"

O Doctor, dear Doctor,
O Doctor de Jongh,
Your Cod Liver Oil
Is so pure and so strong,
I declare to my life,
I'll go down in the soil,
If my wife don't stop drinking
Your Cod Liver Oil.

The Criminal Element

BRENNAN ON THE MOOR

Anonymous

*Willie Brennan operated mainly in the Kilworth mountains region of Co.
Cork. He was a kind of Robin Hood figure and was hanged in 1804.*

It's of a fearless highwayman a story now I'll tell:
His name was Willie Brennan, and in Ireland he did dwell;
'Twas on the Kilworth mountains he commenced his wild career,
Where many a wealthy gentleman before him shook with fear;
Brennan on the moor, Brennan on the moor,
Bold and yet undaunted stood young Brennan on the moor.

A brace of loaded pistols he carried night and day,
He never robb'd a poor man upon the King's highway;
But what he's taken from the rich, like Turpin and Queen Bess,
He always did divide it with the widow in distress.

One night he robbed a packman, his name was Pedlar Bawn;
They travelled on together, till day began to dawn;
The pedlar seeing his money gone, likewise his watch and chain,
He at once encountered Brennan and robbed him back again.

When Brennan saw the pedlar was as good a man as he,
He took him on the highway, his companion for to be;
The pedlar threw away his pack without any more delay,
And proved a faithful comrade until his dying day.

One day upon the highway Willie he sat down,
He met the Mayor of Cashel, a mile outside the town;
The Mayor he knew his features, "I think, young man," said he,
"Your name is Willie Brennan, you must come along with me."

As Brennan's wife had gone to town provisions for to buy,
When she saw her Willie, she began to weep and cry;
He says, "Give me that tenpence;" as soon as Willie spoke,
She handed him the blunderbuss from underneath her cloak.

Then with his loaded blunderbuss, the truth I will unfold,
He made the Mayor to tremble, and robbed him of his gold;
One hundred pounds was offered for his apprehension there,
And with his horse and saddle to the mountains did repair.

Then Brennan being an outlaw upon the mountain high,
Where cavalry and infantry to take him they did try,
He laughed at them with scorn, until at length, it's said,
By a false-hearted young man he was basely betrayed.

In the County of Tipperary, in a place they called Clonmore,
Willie Brennan and his comrade that day did suffer sore;
He lay among the fern which was thick upon the field,
And nine wounds he had received before that he did yield.

Then Brennan and his companion knowing they were betrayed,
He with the mounted cavalry a noble battle made;
He lost his foremost finger, which was shot off by a ball;
So Brennan and his comrade they were taken after all.

So they were taken prisoners, in irons they were bound,
And conveyed to Clonmel jail, strong walls did them surround;
They were tried and found guilty, the judge made this reply.
"For robbing on the King's highway you are both condemned to
    die."

Farewell unto my wife, and to my children three,
Likewise my aged father, he may shed tears for me.
And to my loving mother, who tore her grey locks and cried,
Saying "I wish, Willie Brennan, in your cradle you had died."

Young Molly Bán

Anonymous

Eighteenth-century ballad of the accidental shooting of a sweetheart.
Nowadays he would still have been "set free by the laws of the land"
but he'd be the cops' chief suspect.

Come all you young fellows that follow the gun,
Beware of goin' a-shootin' by the late setting sun.
It might happen to anyone as it happened to me,
To shoot your own true love in-under a tree.

She was going to her uncle's, when the shower it came on,
She went under a bush, the rain for to shun.
With her apron all around her, I took her for a swan
And I levelled my gun and I shot Molly Ban.

I ran to her uncle's in haste and great fear,
Saying Uncle, dear Uncle, I've shot Molly dear.
With her apron all around her I took her for a swan,
But oh and alas! it was my Molly Ban.

I shot my own true love—alas I'm undone,
While she was in the shade by the setting of the sun;
If I thought she was there I'd caress her tenderly,
And soon I'd get married to my own dear Molly.

My curses on you, Toby, that lent me your gun
To go out a-shooting by the late setting sun,
I rubbed her fair temples and found she was dead;
A fountain of tears for my Molly I shed.

Up comes my father and his locks they were grey,
Stay in your own country and don't run away,
Stay in your own country till your trial comes on,
And I'll see you set free by the laws of the land.

Oh the maids of this country they will all be very glad
When they hear the sad news that my Molly is dead.
Take them all in their hundreds, set them all in a row,
Molly Ban she shone above them like a mountain of snow.

THE WILD COLONIAL BOY

Anonymous

Jack Doolan was, like Ned Kelly, a bushranger of Irish extraction. He lived and marauded in Victoria State in the early part of the nineteenth century. Castlemaine is a small town that was once a centre of goldmining, and Beechworth, an even smaller town, lies on the main road from Melbourne to Sydney.

'Tis of a wild Colonial boy, Jack Doolan was his name,
Of poor but honest parents he was born in Castlemaine.
He was his father's only hope, his mother's only joy,
And dearly did his parents love the wild Colonial boy.

Chorus
Come, all my hearties, we'll roam the mountains high,
Together we will plunder, together we will die.
We'll wander over valleys, and gallop over plains,
And we'll scorn to live in slavery, bound down with iron
    chains.

He was scarcely sixteen years of age when he left his father's
    home,
And through Australia's sunny clime a bushranger did roam.
He robbed those wealthy squatters, their stock he did destroy,
And a terror to Australia was the wild Colonial boy.

In sixty-one this daring youth commenced his wild career,
With a heart that knew no danger, no foeman did he fear.
He stuck up the Beechworth mail-coach, and robbed Judge
    MacEvoy,
Who trembled, and gave up his gold to the wild Colonial boy.

He bade the judge "Good morning," and told him to beware,
That he'd never rob a hearty chap that acted on the square,
And never to rob a mother of her son and only joy,
Or else you may turn outlaw, like the wild Colonial boy.

One day as he was riding the mountain-side along,
A-listening to the little birds, their pleasant laughing song,
Three mounted troopers rode along—Kelly, Davis, and FitzRoy—
They thought that they would capture him, the wild Colonial boy.

"Surrender now, Jack Doolan, you see there's three to one.
Surrender now, Jack Doolan, you daring highwayman."
He drew a pistol from his belt, and shook the little toy.
"I'll fight, but not surrender," said the wild Colonial boy.

He fired at Trooper Kelly and brought him to the ground,
And in return from Davis received a mortal wound.
All shattered through the jaws he lay still firing at FitzRoy,
And that's the way they captured him—the wild Colonial boy.

WILLIE REILLY

Anonymous

One of William Carleton's mother's favourite songs and based upon a true story which Carleton turned into a novel in 1855 as Willie Reilly and his dear Cooleen Bawn. *It was one of Joxer Daly's favourite books. The "Coolen Ban" was Helen Foillard, a fair-haired Orangewoman who connived at her abduction by her Catholic lover. The directness of the narrative and the implication that the audience knew the story as well as the balladeer are characteristic of the broadsheet ballad as sung and sold at fairs.*

"Oh! rise up, Willie Reilly, and come along with me,
I mean for to go with you and leave this counterie,
To leave my father's dwelling, his houses and free land;"
And away goes Willie Reilly and his dear Coolen Ban.

They go by hills and mountains and by yon lonesome plain,
Through shady groves and valleys all danger to refrain;
But her father followed after with a well-armed band,
And taken was poor Reilly and his dear Coolen Ban.

It's home then she was taken, and in her closet bound;
Poor Reilly all in Sligo gaol lay on the stony ground.
Till at the bar of justice, before the Judge he'd stand,
For nothing but the stealing of his dear Coolen Ban.

"Now in the cold, cold iron my hands and feet are bound,
I'm handcuffed like a murderer, and tied unto the ground.
But all the toil and slavery I'm willing for to stand,
Still hoping to be succoured by my dear Coolen Ban."

The Gaoler's son to Reilly goes and thus to him did say,
"Oh, get up, Willie Reilly, you must appear this day,
For great Squire Foillard's anger you never can withstand,
I'm afeard you'll suffer sorely for your dear Coolen Ban.

"This is the news, young Reilly, last night that I did hear:
The lady's oath will hang you or else will set you clear."
"If that be so," says Reilly, "her pleasure I will stand,
Still hoping to be succoured by my dear Coolen Ban."

Now Willie's dressed from top to toe all in a suit of green;
His hair hangs o'er his shoulders most glorious to be seen;
He's tall and straight and comely as any could be found;
He's fit for Foillard's daughter, were she heiress to a crown.

The Judge he said: "This lady being in her tender youth,
If Reilly had deluded her she will declare the truth,"
Then, like a moving beauty bright, before him she did stand,
"You're welcome there, my heart's delight and dear Coolen Ban."

"Oh gentlemen," Squire Foillard said, "with pity look on me,
This villain came amongst us to disgrace our family,
And by his base contrivances this villainy was planned;
If I don't get satisfaction I'll quit this Irish land."

The lady with a tear began, and thus replied she:
"The fault is none of Reilly's, the blame lies all on me;
I forced him for to leave his place and come along with me;
I loved him out of measure, which wrought our destiny."

Out bespoke the noble Fox at the table he stood by:
"Oh, gentlemen, consider on this extremity;
To hang a man for love is a murder you may see:
So spare the life of Reilly, let him leave this counterie."

"Good my lord, he stole from her her diamonds and her rings,
Gold watch and silver buckles, and many precious things,
Which cost me in bright guineas more than five hundred
    pounds,
I'll have the life of Reilly should I lose ten thousand pounds."

"Good my Lord, I gave them him as tokens of true love,
And when we are a-parting I will them all remove;
If you have got them, Reilly, pray send them home to me."
"I will, my loving lady, with many thanks to thee."

"There is a ring among them I allow yourself to wear,
With thirty locket diamonds well set in silver fair,
And as a true-love token wear it on your right hand,
That you'll think on my poor broken heart when you're in
    foreign land."

Then out spoke noble Fox: "You may let the prisoner go;
The lady's oath has cleared him, as the jury all may know.
She has released her own true love, she has renewed his name;
May her honour bright gain high estate and her offspring rise
    to fame!"

THE LAMENTATION OF HUGH REYNOLDS

Anonymous

An "execution" ballad from Co. Cavan and one of the first to use the resonant Gaelic pun on "dear." Catherine McCabe was the main prosecution witness in the charge of breaking and entering, then a capital offence. The execution was set for 28 March 1826 in Cavan Town but the perjury was discovered and Reynolds was set free.

My name it is Hugh Reynolds I came of honest parents,
Near Cavan I was born as you may plainly see
For the loving of a maid one Catherine McCabe
My life has been betrayed she's the dear maid to me—

The country was bewailing my doleful situation
But still I'd expectation this maid would set me free—
But O, she was ungrateful, her parents prov'd deceitful
An' tho' I lov'd her faithful, she's the dear maid to me.

Young men and tender maidens, throughout this Irish
    nation,
Who hear my lamentation, I hope you'll pray for me;
The truth I will unfold, that my precious blood she sold,
In the grave I must lie cold; she's the dear maid to me.

For now my glass is run, my last hour it is come,
And I must die for love and the height of loyalty!
I thought it was no harm to embrace her in my arms,
Or take her from her parents; but she's the dear maid to me.

Adieu, my loving father, and you, my tender mother,
Farewell, my dearest brother, who has suffered sore for me;
With irons I'm surrounded, in grief I lie confounded,
By perjury unbounded; she's the dear maid to me.

Now, I can say no more; to the Law-board I must go,
There to take my last farewell of my friends and counterie;
May the angels, shining bright, receive my soul this night,
And convey me into heaven with the blessed Trinity.

The Sorrowful Lamentation of Callaghan, Greally, and Mullen, Killed at the Fair of Turloughmore

Anonymous

A street ballad describing the results when on 1 August 1843 at the fair of Darrynacloughery near Turloughmore, Co. Galway during rioting after a faction fight the police fired into the crowd. The "Brew" in verse six was the stipendiary magistrate whose order the police used to justify the measure. He died the day before the hearing.

"Come tell me, dearest mother, what makes my father stay,
Or what can be the reason that he's so long away?"
"Oh! hold your tongue, my darling son, your tears do grieve
    me sore,
I fear he has been murdered in the fair of Turloughmore."

Come, all you tender Christians, I hope you will draw near,
It's of this dreadful murder I mean to let you hear,
Concerning those poor people whose loss we do deplore—
(The Lord have mercy on their souls) that died at
    Turloughmore.

It is on the First of August, the truth I will declare,
Those people they assembled that day all at the fair;
But little was their notion what evil was in store,
All by the bloody Peelers at the fair of Turloughmore.

Were you to see that dreadful sight it would grieve your heart I
    know,
To see the comely women and the men all lying low;
God help their tender parents, they will never see them more,
For cruel was their murder at the fair of Turloughmore.

It's for that base blood-thirsty crew, remark the word I say,
The Lord he will reward them against the judgment-day,
The blood they have taken innocent for it they'll suffer sore,
And the treatment that they gave to us that day at Turloughmore.

The morning of their trial as they stood up in the dock,
The words they spoke were feeling, the people round them flock,
"I tell you Judge and Jury, the truth I will declare,
It was Brew that ordered us to fire that evening at the fair."

Now to conclude and finish this sad and doleful fray,
I hope their souls are happy against the judgment-day,
It was little time they got to know, when they fell like new-
    mowed hay,
May the Lord have mercy on their souls against the judgment-
    day.

THE BOSTON BURGLAR

Anonymous

*Like "The Wild Colonial Boy" still firmly in the Irish tradition,
though set beyond the sea.*

> I was born and bred in Boston,
> A place you all know well,
> Brought up by honest parents,
> The truth to you I'll tell,
> Brought up by honest parents,
> And reared most tenderly,
> Till I became a sporty boy
> At the age of twenty-three.
>
> My character was broken,
> And I was sent to jail,
> My friends and parents did their best
> To get me out on bail,
> But the jury found me guilty
> And the judge he wrote it down
> "For the breaking of the Union Bank
> You are sent to Charlestown."
>
> I can see my dear old father
> Standing at the bar,
> Also my own dear mother
> Was tearing out her hair,
> Tearing out her old grey locks
> And the tears came tumbling down,
> "My son, my son, what have you done
> To be sent to Charlestown?"

I set my foot on an east going train
One cold December day,
In every station I passed by
I could hear the people say
"There goes the Boston Burglar
In strong irons he is bound
For the breaking of the Union Bank,
He is sent to Charlestown."

There's a girl in Boston City,
A girl that I know well,
And if e'er I get my liberty
With her I mean to dwell,
If e'er I get my liberty
Rough company I will shun,
Likewise the walking of the streets,
Likewise the drinking of rum.

Now you that have your liberty
Pray keep it if you can
And don't go midnight rambling
Or you'll break the laws of man,
And if you do you're sure to rue
And you will find yourself like me,
A sentenced down to twenty years
Of Penal Servitee.

Van Diemen's Land

Anonymous

A ballad from before 1853 (when transportation was abolished). The Tipperary poachers were unusually unlucky in being sent to Tasmania, a destination usually reserved for political offenders. The off-shore Australian state was actually discovered by Abel Tasman in 1642 and named in honour of his patron, the governor-general of Batavia.

Come all you gallant poachers that ramble void of care,
That walk out on a moonlight night with your dog and gun and
    snare.
The hare and lofty pheasant you have at your command,
Not thinking of your last career upon Van Diemen's Land.

Poor Thomas Brown from Nenagh town, Jack Murphy and poor
    Joe
Were three determined poachers as the country well does know
By the keepers of the land, my boys, one night they were
    trepanned
And for fourteen years transported unto Van Diemen's Land.

The first day that we landed upon that fatal shore
The planters came around us, there might be twenty score.
They ranked us off like horses and they sold us out of hand
And they yoked us to the plough, brave boys, to plough Van
    Diemen's Land.

The cottages we live in are built with sods of clay
We have rotten straw for bedding but we dare not say nay.
Our cots we fence with firing and slumber when we can
To keep the wolves and tigers from us in Van Diemen's Land.

Oft times when I do slumber I have a pleasant dream
With my sweet girl sitting near me close by a purling stream;
I am roaming through old Ireland with my true love by the hand,
But awaken broken-hearted upon Van Diemen's Land.

God bless our wives and families, likewise that happy shore,
That isle of sweet contentment which we shall ne'er see more;
As for the wretched families see them we seldom can;
There are twenty men for one woman in Van Diemen's Land.

There was a girl from Nenagh town, Peg Brophy was her name,
For fourteen years transported was, we all well knew the same;
But our planter bought her freedom and married her out of hand
And she gives to us good usage upon Van Diemen's Land.

But fourteen years is a long time, that is our fatal doom,
For nothing else but poaching for that is all we done;
You would leave off both dog and gun and poaching every man
If you but knew the hardship that's in Van Diemen's Land.

Oh, if I had a thousand pounds all laid out in my hand,
I'd give it all for liberty if that I could command,
Again to Ireland I'd return and be a happy man
And bid adieu to poaching and to Van Diemen's Land.

The Night before Larry was Stretched

Anonoymous

A famous and valuable relic of early Dublin lowlife. The odd expressions are thieves' cant: "sweated their duds" for example means "pawned their clothes." The last verse with the "numbing chit" (gallows) and the "rumbler" (cart) is a chilling reminder that in the days before the use of the trap-door the condemned man died slowly of strangulation. Friends used to swing from his feet to hasten the end. The poem is attributed to Robert Burrows, the rackety Dean of Cork, though other authorities say it was created by William Maher ("Hurlfoot Bill"). It dates from 1816.

The night before Larry was stretched,
The boys they all paid him a visit;
A bit in their sacks, too, they fetched;
They sweated their duds till they riz it;
For Larry was ever the lad,
When a boy was condemned to the squeezer,
Would fence all the duds that he had
To help a poor friend to a sneezer,
And warm his gob 'fore he died.

The boys they came crowding in fast,
They drew all their stools round about him,
Six glims round his trap-case were placed,
He couldn't be well waked without 'em.
When one of us asked could he die
Without having truly repented,
Says Larry, "That's all in my eye,
And first by the clergy invented,
To get a fat bit for themselves."

"I'm sorry, dear Larry," says I,
"To see you in this situation;
And, blister my limbs if I lie,
I'd as lieve it had been my own station."
"Ochone! it's all over," says he,
"For the neck-cloth I'll be forced to put on,
And by this time tomorrow you'll see
Your poor Larry as dead as a mutton,
Because why, his courage was good.

"And I'll be cut up like a pie,
And my nob from my body be parted."
"You're in the wrong box, then," says I,
"For blast me if they're so hard-hearted;
A chalk on the back of your neck
Is all that Jack Ketch dares to give you;
Then mind not such trifles a feck,
For why should the likes of them grieve you?
And now, boys, come tip us the deck."

The cards being called for, they played,
Till Larry found one of them cheated;
A dart at his napper he made
(The boy being easily heated);
"O, by the hokey, you thief,
I'll scuttle your nob with my daddle!
You cheat me because I'm in grief,
But soon I'll demolish your noddle,
And leave you your claret to drink."

Then the clargy came in with his book,
He spoke him so smooth and so civil;
Larry pitched him a Kilmainham look,
And pitched his big wig to the devil;
Then sighing, he threw back his head,
To get a sweet drop of the bottle,
And pitiful sighing, he said:
"Oh, the hemp will be soon round my throttle,
And choke my poor windpipe to death.

"Though sure it's the best way to die,
O! the devil a better a-livin'!
For when the gallows is high
Your journey is shorter to heaven:
But what harasses Larry the most,
And makes his poor soul melancholy,
Is that he thinks of the time when his ghost
Will come in a sheet to poor Molly;
O, sure it will kill her alive!"

So moving these last words he spoke,
We all vented our tears in a shower;
For my part, I thought my heart broke,
To see him cut down like a flower.
On his travels we watched him next day;
O! the throttler, I thought I could kill him;
But Larry not one word did say,
Nor changed till he came to King William,
Then, musha, his colour grew white.

When we came to the numbing chit,
He was tucked up so neat and so pretty,
The rumbler jogged off from his feet,
And he died with his face to the city;
He kicked, too—but that was all pride,
For soon you might see 'twas all over;
Soon after the noose was untied,
And at darkee we waked him in clover,
And sent him to take a ground sweat.

About the Country

COME TO THE BOWER

Anonymous

Early tour of Erin, anticipating the worst efforts of Bord Fáilte.

Will you come to the bow'r o'er the free boundless ocean
Where the stupendous waves roll in thunderin' motion
Where the mermaids are seen and the fierce tempest gathers.
To lov'd Erin the Green the dear land of our fathers,
Will you come, will you, will you, will you come to the Bower?

Will you come to the land of O'Neill and O'Donnell
Of Lord Lucan of old and the immortal O'Connell.
Where Brian drove the Danes and St. Patrick the vermin
And whose valleys remain still most beautiful and charming.

You can visit Benburb and the storied Black Water,
Where Owen Roe met Munroe and his chieftains did slaughter
Where the lambs skip and play on the mossey all over,
From those bright golden views to enchanting Rostrevor.

You can see Dublin City and the fine groves of Blarney,
The Bann, Boyne, the Liffey and the Lakes of Killarney;
You may ride on the tide o'er the broad majestic Shannon,
You may sail round Loch Neagh and see storied Dungannon.

You can visit New Ross, gallant Wexford and Gorey,
Where the green was last seen by proud Saxon and Tory,
Where the soil is sanctified by the blood of each true man
Where they died satisfied their enemies they would not run
    from.

Will you come and awake our lost land from its slumber
And her fetters we will break, links that long are encumbered,
And the air will resound with Hosanna to greet you
On the shore will be found gallant Irishmen to meet you.

Will you come, will you, will you, will you come to the Bower?

THE BANKS OF CLAUDY

Anonymous

Early nineteenth-century song from County Derry with the common motif of the lover returning in disguise. Unusually this one ends happily.

It was on a summer's morning all in the month of May
Down by the banks of Claudy I carelessly did stray
I overheard a female in sorrow to complain
All for her absent lover that ploughed the raging main.

I stepped up unto her and gave her a surprise—
I own she did not know me, I being in disguise.
I says "My fairest creature, my joy and heart's delight,
How far do you mean to wander this dark and dreary night?"

"It's to the banks of Claudy, if you'll be pleased to show;
Take pity on a fair maid who knows not where to go.
I'm searching for a young man, and Johnny is his name,
And on the banks of Claudy I'm told he does remain."

"These are the banks of Claudy, fair maid, whereon you stand;
But do not trust your Johnny, for he's a false young man,
But do not trust young Johnny, for he'll not meet you here,
But tarry with me in green woods, no danger need you fear."

"If Johnny was here this night he would keep me from all harm,
But he's in the field of battle, all in his uniform;
He's in the field of battle, and his foes he does defy,
Like the royal king of honour all on the walls of Troy."

"It is six long weeks or better since Johnny left this shore
A-crossing the main ocean, where thundering billows roar;
A-crossing the main ocean for honour and for fame,
But I am told the ship was wrecked nigh to the coast of Spain."

O, when she heard this dreadful news she flew in deep despair;
A wringing of her hands and a tearing of her hair,
Saying: "If my Johnny's drownéd no man alive I'll take,
Through lonesome shades and valleys I'll wander for his sake."

When he saw her loyalty no longer could he stand:
He flew into her arms, saying, "Betsey, I'm the man,"
Saying "Betsey, I'm the young man, the cause of all your pain;
Now, since we've met on Claudy banks we'll never part again."

KITTY OF COLERAINE

Charles Dawson Shanly or Edward Lysaght

If ever a poem fulfilled the definition of telling a story and being able to be sung this one does. It is as fresh now as when it was written. But by whom? Probably by Lysaght because of its Georgian prettiness. It also served to give Coleraine some badly needed literary respectability.

As beautiful Kitty one morning was tripping
With a pitcher of milk for the fair of Coleraine,
Whe she saw me she stumbled, the pitcher down tumbled,
And all the sweet buttermilk watered the plain.
"Oh, what shall I do now? 'Twas looking at you now!
I'm sure such a pitcher I'll ne'er see again.
'Twas the pride of my dairy. Oh, Barney McCleary,
You're sent as a plague to the girls of Coleraine."

I sat down beside her, and gently did chide her
That such a misfortune should give her such pain;
A kiss then I gave her, and before I did leave her
She vowed for such pleasure she'd break it again.
'Twas the haymaking season—I can't tell the reason—
Misfortunes will never come single, 'tis plain!
For very soon after poor Kitty's disaster
The devil a pitcher was whole in Coleraine.

THE MAID OF THE SWEET BROWN KNOWE

Anonymous

A type of ballad known in the north as a "Come-all-ye" because of the many that began with the words, "Come all ye lads and lassies…" It is associated with the Sperrin Mountains and repeats a common theme: the fate of teasing lovers who miss their chances.

Come all ye lads and lassies and listen to me awhile,
And I'll sing for you a verse or two will cause you all to smile;
It's all about a young man, and I'm going to tell you now,
How he lately came a-courting of the Maid of the Sweet Brown
    Knowe.

Said he, "My pretty fair maid, will you come along with me,
We'll both go off together, and married we will be;
We'll join our hands in wedlock bands, I'm speaking to you now,
And I'll do my best endeavour for the Maid of the Sweet Brown
    Knowe."

This fair and fickle young thing, she knew not what to say,
Her eyes did shine like silver bright and merrily did play;
She said, "Young man, your love subdue, for I am not ready now,
And I'll spend another season at the foot of the Sweet Brown
    Knowe."

Said he, "My pretty fair maid how can you say so,
Look down in yonder valley where my crops do gently grow,
Look down in yonder valley where my horses and my plough
Are at their daily labour for the Maid of the Sweet Brown
    Knowe."

"If they're at their daily labour, kind sir, it's not for me,
For I've heard of your behaviour, I have, indeed," said she;
"There is an Inn where you call in, I have heard the people say,
Where you rap and call and pay for all, and go home at the break
   of day."

"If I rap and call and pay for all, the money is all my own,
And I'll never spend your fortune, for I hear you have got none.
You thought you had my poor heart broke in talking with me
   now,
But I'll leave you where I found you, at the foot of the Sweet
   Brown Knowe."

MOORLUG MARY

Anonymous

Strictly speaking the title should be "Moor Lough Mary" from the circular lake in the western Sperrins near Strabane. The Mourne is the name given to that part of the River Foyle between the tributaries Finn and Derg.

The first I saw of my Moorlug Mary
Was on the fair day of sweet Strabane,
Her smiling face it was so engaging,
All other fair maids she did trepan,
Her killing eyes—sure they have me blinded,
No rest I find either night or day,
From quiet slumber I rise in wonder,
Saying "Moorlug Mary, will you come away?"

From Moorlug banks I will never wander,
Where heifers graze on yon pleasant hill;
Where lambkins sporting, fair maids resorting,
The timorous hare and blue heather bell.
I'll press my cheese, and my wool I'll tease,
And my ewes I'll milk by the eve of day;
The hurling moor-cock and lark allures me;
From bonnie Moorlug I'll never stray.

I'll go down yon woodland to my situation,
Where recreation is all in view,
On the river Mourne where the salmon sporting,
And echoes sounding bring something new.

The thrush and goldfinch will join in chorus
With notes melodious on Liskea Brae,
To the sweet Loch shore then I would restore you,
Saying, "Moorlug Mary, will you come away?"

Were I a man of great education,
And Ireland's nation at my command.
I'd lay my head on her snowy shoulder,
In wedlock's portion I'd take her hand,
I'd entertain her both eve and morning;
With robes I'd deck her both rich and gay;
With kisses fragrant I would embrace her,
Saying, "Moorlug Mary, will you come away?"

THE FLOWER OF SWEET STRABANE

Anonymous

Another nostalgic nineteenth-century song of lost love and forcible emigration, with a tribute to the beauty of the women of a very friendly town.

Were I the King of Ireland with all things at my will,
I would roam for recreation, new comforts to find still,
But the comfort I would like best you all may understand,
Is to win the heart of Martha, the flower of sweet Strabane.

Her cheeks are like the roses red, her hair a lovely brown,
And o'er her milk-white shoulders it carelessly hangs down.
She's one of the finest creatures of the whole Milesian clan,
Oh, my heart is fairly captured by the flower of sweet Strabane.

I wish I had my darling far down in Inishowen,
Or in some lonely valley in the wild woods of Tyrone.
I would do my best endeavour, I would work the newest plan,
To gain the heart of Martha, the flower of sweet Strabane.

I've often been in Phoenix Park, and in Killarney fair,
In blithe and bonnie Scotland, on the winding banks of Ayr;
But yet in all my travels I never met with one
That could compare with Martha, the flower of sweet Strabane.

But since I cannot win your love, no joy there is for me.
So I will seek forgetfulness in lands across the sea;
Unless you chance to follow me, I swear by my right han',
Macdonald's face you'll never see, fair flower of sweet Strabane.

Adieu, then, to the Liffey's banks, and Mourne's water's side.
I'm sailing for America, whatever may betide;
Our ship is bound for Liverpool, straight by the Isle of Man,
Adieu, my dearest Martha, the flower of sweet Strabane.

THE MUTTONBURN STREAM

Anonymous

Stream near Carrickfergus, Co. Antrim with near-magical properties.
Its tribute was still being sung in the town forty years ago.

I remember my young days when younger I've been,
I remember my young days by the Muttonburn Stream,
It's not marked on this world's map, it's nowhere to be seen,
A wee river in Ulster, the Muttonburn Stream.

It flows through the bridges, takes many's a turn,
It turns round the mill wheel that grinds the folks' corn,
It flows through the meadows, it keeps the land clean,
Belfast Lough it soon reaches, the Muttonburn Stream.

Now the ducks like to swim in it from morning to eve,
Though they dirty the water they make themselves clean.
I have seen them a-diving till their tails scarce was seen,
Waddling down to the bottom of the Muttonburn Stream.

The ladies from Carrick I oftimes have seen,
Bringing down their wee washing to the Muttonburn Stream,
No powder nor soap used, a wee dunt makes them clean,
It has great cleansing power, the Muttonburn Stream.

And it cures all diseases, though chronic they've been,
It will cure you of fatness, or cure you of lean,
Sure the 'jaundies' itself now, weak heart, or strong spleen,
All give way to the power of the Muttonburn Stream.

A-partying at night-time when I'd not be seen,
They give great fine parties that live round the stream,
Comin' home in the morning so gay and serene,
Sure I tripped and I fell in the Muttonburn Stream.

THE QUEEN OF CONNEMARA

Frank A. Fahy

Tribute to a Connacht queen by the man who founded the London Gaelic League.

Oh! my boat can swiftly float
In the teeth of wind and weather,
And outsail the fastest hooker
Between Galway and Kinsale.
When the white rim of the ocean
And the wild waves rush together—
Oh, she rides in her pride
Like a seabird in a gale.

Chorus
She's neat, oh, she's sweet;
She's a beauty in every line—
The Queen of Connemara
Is this bounding barque of mine.

When she's loaded down with fish,
'Til the water lips the gunwale,
Not a drop she'll take abroad her
That would wash a fly away;
From the fleet she speeds out quickly
Like a greyhound from her kennel,
'Till she lands her silvery store the first
On old Kinvara Quay.
Chorus

There's a light shines out afar
And it keeps me from dismaying—
When the clouds are ink above us,
And the sea runs white with foam,
In a cot in Connemara
There's a wife and wee ones praying
To the One Who walked the waters once
To bring us safely home.
Chorus

THE FLOWER OF MAGHERALLY

Anonymous
Typical topographical ballad: there is hardly a village or townland in Ireland which cannot advance its own example.

It was on a summer's morning
When flowers were a-blooming, O,
When meadows were adorning,
And small birds sweetly tuning, O,
I met my love near Banbridge Town,
My charming blooming Sally, O,
And she is the crown of County Down,
The Flow'r of Magherally, O.

With admiration I did gaze
Upon this blooming maiden, O;
Adam never was more struck
When he first saw Eve in Eden, O;
Her skin was like the lily white,
That grows in yonder valley, O;
And I thinks I'm blest when I am nigh
The Flower of Magherally, O.

Her yellow hair in ringlets fell,
Her shoes were Spanish leather, O,
Her bonnet with blue ribbons strung,
Her scarlet scarf and feather, O.
Like Venus bright she did appear,
My charming blooming Sally, O.
And she is the girl that I love dear,
The Flower of Magherally, O.

An Irish lad although I be,
With neither wealth nor treasure, O;
But yet I love my dearest dear,
I love her beyond measure, O.
If I'd all the wealth that is possessed
By the great Titharally, O;
I'd give it to her that I love best,
The Flower of Magherally, O.

But I hope the time will surely come,
When we'll join hands together, O;
It's then I'll take my darling home,
In spite of wind and weather, O.
And let them all say what they will,
And let them scowl and rally, O;
For I shall wed the girl I love,
The Flower of Magherally, O.

A New Song on the Rocks of Baun

Anonymous

The sorrows of both master and man when they are ill-matched. Internal evidence puts the date as during Victoria's reign. The suggestion that army life is preferable to being a hireling makes it later rather than early in the century.

Come all you loyal heroes wherever that you be,
Don't hire with any master till you know what your work will be,
For you must rise up early from the clear day-light till dawn,
I'm afraid you won't be able for to plough the Rocks of Baun.

My shoes they are well worn now and my stockings they are
    thin,
My heart is always trembling afeared that I'd give in,
My heart is nearly broken from the clear daylight till dawn,
And I never will be able for to plough the rocks of Baun.

My curse attend you, Sweeney, for you have me nearly robbed,
You're sitting by the fireside with your feet upon the hob,
You're sitting by the fireside from the clear daylight till dawn,
But you never will be able for to plough the rocks of Baun.

O rise up, lovely Sweeney, and give your horse its hay,
And give him a good feed of oats before you start away,
Don't feed him on soft turnips, take him down to your green
    lawn,
And then you might be able for to plough the rocks of Baun.

I wish the Queen of England would write to me in time,
And place me in some regiment all in my youth and prime,
I'd fight for Ireland's glory from the clear daylight till dawn,
And I never would return again to plough the rocks of Baun.

The Newry Prentice Boy

Anonymous

Old song of the boss's daughter and the likely lad. It is easy to understand the father's concern.

Come all you happy lovers I pray you lend an ear,
And listen to those few verses that I have wrote in fear,
Concerning of a weaver lad and him apprentice bound,
And I myself an heiress of thirty thousand pound.

O me and him in the garden stood inunder a greenwood tree,
He took me in his arms and he used me tenderly;
We both sat down in a shady bower for to converse our joy,
How sweetly sing the valley's rills with my darling prentice boy.

My father being in the garden, he heard what we did say.
He says, "False maid, let you arise and send your love away."
He says, "False maid, let you arise, I'll deprive you of your joy."
Let him say as he will, I love him still, my darling prentice boy.

O lay me in the laurel tree, of it I'll make my bed,
The sycamore leaves and juniper will shade my weary bed;
Till he returns to live with me no man will I enjoy,
Let him go where he will, I love him still, my darling prentice
    boy.

The Turfman from Ardee

Anonymous

A Co Louth encounter. The title is much better known than the actual song, which dates from the late 1830s.

For sake of health I took a walk last week at early dawn.
I met a jolly turfman as I slowly jogged along.
The kindest salutations passed 'twixt him and me.
And it's soon I got acquainted with the Turfman from Ardee.

We chatted very freely as we jogged along the road
He says, "My ass is tired, and I want to sell my load,
For I've got no refreshment since I left my home you see
I am wearied out with travelling," says the Turfman from Ardee.

"Your cart is racked and worn friend, your ass is very old,
It must be twenty summers since that animal was foaled."
"He was yoked in a trap when I was born, September, '83,
And he cantered for the midwife," says the Turfman from
    Ardee.

"I own my cart, it must be made of the very best of wood,
I do believe it was in use the time of Noah's flood.
The axle never wanted grease but one year out of three—
It's a real old Carrick axle," says the Turfman from Ardee.

"I often do abuse the beast with this rough hazel rod,
Although I own I never yet did drive poor Jack unshod.
The harness now that's on his back was made by John Magee,
Who's dead this two and forty years," says the Turfman from
    Ardee.

We talked about our country's woes and how we were oppressed,
The men we sent to Parliament to get our wrongs redressed,
"Sure, all these politicians are nothing else I see,
But led by bloomin' humbug," says the Turfman from Ardee.

Just then I heard a female voice that I knew very well,
Politely asking this old man his load of turf to sell.
I shook that horny hand of his and bowed respectfully,
In hopes to meet some future day the Turfman from Ardee.

Exiles' Laments

THE GIRL I LEFT BEHIND ME

Anonymous

*A British Army tune still used as a march past which was imported
and Irished at the end of the eighteenth century. As with the original
song placenames could be changed without too much injury to metre.*

Come all ye handsome comely maids
That live near Carlow dwelling
Beware of young men's flatt'ring tongue,
When love to you they're telling
Beware of the kind words they say,
Be wise and do not mind them,
For if they were talking till they die
They'd leave you all behind them.

In Carlow town I lived I own
All free from debt and danger.
Till Colonel Reilly listed me
To join the Wicklow Rangers.
They dressed me up in scarlet red
And they used me very kindly
But still I thought my heart would break
For the girl I left behind me.

I was scarcely fourteen years of age
When I was broken-hearted
For I'm in love these two long years
Since from my love I parted
These maidens wonder how I moan
And bid me not to mind him
That he might have more grief than joy
For leaving me behind him.

So now my love is gone from me
I own I do not blame him
For oftentimes he told to me
That he never would deceive me
But now he's gone across the foam
Unto some distant island
But in course of time he may come home
To the girl he left behind him.

'Tis not my love I claim I own
All for our separation
That left me wandering far from home
All in a distant station
But when e'er I get my liberty
No man shall ever bind me
I'll see my native land once more
And the girl I left behind me.

GOOD BYE MURSHEEN DURKIN

Anonymous

Ballad of a disaffected Munster man who in 1849 preferred the goldfields of California to the potato gardens of home.

In the days I went a-courtin,
I was never tired resortin,
to the alehouse and the play house, and many a house beside,
But I told me brother Seamus,
I'll be off now and grow famous,
And before I come home again, I'll roam the world wide.

O! I courted girls in Blarney,
In Kanturk and Killarney,
In Passage and in Queenstown, I mean the Cove of Cork;
But I'm tired of all this pleasure,
So now I'll take my leisure,
And the next time that you hear, 'twill be a letter from New York.

So good-bye Mursheen Durkin,
Sure, I'm sick and tired of workin',
No more I'll dig the praties, no longer I'll be fooled:
But as sure as my name is Corney
I'll be off to Californy
And instead of diggin' praties, I'll be diggin' lumps of gold.

MARY FROM DUNGLOE

Anonymous

*Late-nineteenth-century exile's lament given a fresh run as the theme
song of the "Mary from Dungloe" festival held in the town each summer.*

Oh, then, fare ye well sweet Donegal, the Rosses and Gweedore
I'm crossing the main ocean, where the foaming billows roar
It breaks my heart from you to part, where I spent many happy
    days—
Farewell to kind relations, for I'm bound for Amerikay.

Oh, my love is tall and handsome and her age is scarce eighteen
She far exceeds all other fair maids when she trips over the
    green
Her lovely neck and shoulders are fairer than the snow
Till the day I die I'll ne'er deny my Mary from Dungloe.

If I was at home in Sweet Dungloe a letter I would write
Kind thoughts would fill my bosom for Mary my delight
'Tis in her father's garden, the fairest violets grow
And 'twas there I came to court the maid, my Mary from
    Dungloe.

Ah then, Mary you're my heart's delight my pride and only care
It was your cruel father, would not let me stray there.
But absence makes the heart grow fond and when I'm o'er the
    main
May the Lord protect my darling girl till I return again.

And I wished I was in sweet Dungloe and seated on the grass
And by my side a bottle of wine and on my knee a lass.
I'd call for liquor of the best and I'd pay before I would go
And I'd roll my Mary in my arms in the town of sweet
    Dungloe.

SLIEVENAMON

Charles J Kickham

One of several songs from the pen of the laureate of Tipperary whose Fenian activism and poor health prevented his settling down in marriage with any of the women he wrote about so poignantly.

Alone, all alone, by the wave-wash'd strand,
And alone in the crowded hall.
The hall it is gay, and the waves they are grand,
But my heart is not here at all!
It flies far away, by night and by day,
To the time and the joys that are gone!
And I never can forget the sweet maiden I met,
In the Valley near Slievenamon.

It was not the grace of her queenly air,
Nor her cheek of the rose's glow,
Nor her soft black eyes, nor her flowing hair,
Nor was it her lily-white brow.
'Twas the soul of truth and of melting ruth,
And the smile like a Summer dawn,
That stole my heart away one soft Summer day,
In the Valley near Slievenamon.

In the festive hall, by the star-watch'd shore,
Ever my restless spirit cries:
"My love, oh, my love, shall I ne'er see you more?
And, my land, will you never uprise?"
By night and by day, I ever, ever, pray,
While lonely my life flows on,
To see our flag unrolled, and my true love to enfold,
In the Valley near Slievenamon.

THE OLD BOG ROAD
Teresa Brayton

This grand old standard of parties of fifty years ago was written at the end of the last century by an exile from Co Kildare.

My feet are here on Broadway this blessed harvest morn,
But O the ache that's in them for the spot where I was born.
My weary hands are blistered from work in cold and heat,
And O to swing a scythe to-day, thro' fields of Irish wheat.
Had I the chance to wander back, or own a king's abode,
'Tis soon I'd see the hawthorn tree by the Old Bog Road.

When I was young and restless, my mind was ill at ease,
Through dreaming of America, and gold beyond the seas,
O sorrow take their money, 'tis hard to get that same,
And what's the world to any man, where no one speaks his name.
I've had my day and here I am, with building bricks for load,
A long three thousand miles away, from the Old Bog Road.

My mother died last spring tide, when Ireland's fields were green,
The neighbours said her waking was the finest ever seen.
There were snowdrops and primroses piled up beside her bed,
And Ferns Church was crowded, when her funeral Mass was said.
But there was I on Broadway, with building bricks for load,
When they carried out her coffin, from the Old Bog Road.

There was a decent girl at home, who used to walk with me,
Her eyes were soft and sorrowful, like sunbeams on the sea,
Her name was Mary Dwyer; but that was long ago,
And the ways of God are wiser, than the things a man may know.
She died the year I left her, with building bricks for load,
I'd best forget the times we met, on the Old Bog Road.

Ah! life's a weary puzzle, past finding out by man,
I take the day for what it's worth and do the best I can.
Since no one cares a rush for me; what needs to make a moan,
I go my way, and draw my pay and smoke my pipe alone,
Each human heart must know its grief, tho' little be its load,
So God be with you Ireland, and the Old Bog Road.

The Moon Behind The Hill

William Keneally

A piece of Kilkenny nostalgia, written by "William of Munster" for
The Nation, *which afterwards became one of the Christy Minstrels*
standards. The minstrels were an American black-faced troupe who
made the songs of Stephen Foster famous.

I watched last night the rising moon,
Upon a foreign strand,
Till mem'ries came like flowers of June,
Of home and fatherland:
I dreamt I was a child once more,
Beside the rippling rill,
When first I saw, in days of yore
The moon behind the hill.

It brought me back the visions grand
That purpled boyhood's dreams,
Its youthful loves, its happy land,
As bright as morning beams;
It brought me back my own sweet Nore.
The castle and the mill,
Until my eyes could see no more
The moon behind the hill.

It brought me back a mother's love,
Until, in accents wild,
I prayed her from her home above
To guard her lonely child;
It brought me one across the wave
To live in mem'ry still:
It brought me back my Kathleen's grave,
The moon behind the hill.

And there, beneath the silv'ry sky
I lived life o'er again;
I counted all its hopes gone by,
I wept at all its pain;
And when I'm gone, oh! may some tongue,
The minstrel's wish fulfil,
And still remember him who sang,
"The Moon behind the Hill."

Old Skibbereen

Anonymous

Famine ballad from west Cork set in the district where the famine of the 1840s was particularly vicious. The town had sufficiently recovered its spirit by 1914 to carry in the local newspaper the headline: "The Skibbereen Eagle has its eye on the Kaiser."

Oh, father dear, I often hear you speak of Erin's Isle,
Her lofty scenes and valleys green, her mountains rude and wild,
They say it is a lovely land wherein a prince might dwell,
Oh, why did you abandon it? the reason to me tell.

Oh, son! I loved my native land with energy and pride,
Till a blight came o'er my crops—my sheep, my cattle died;
My rent and taxes were too high, I could not them redeem,
And that's the cruel reason that I left old Skibbereen.

Oh, well do I remember the bleak December day,
The landlord and the sheriff came to drive us all away;
They set my roof on fire with their cursed English spleen,
And that's another reason that I left old Skibbereen.

Your mother, too, God rest her soul, fell on the snowy ground,
She fainted in her anguish, seeing the desolation round,
She never rose, but passed away from life to mortal dream,
And found a quiet grave, my boy, in dear old Skibbereen.

And you were only two years old and feeble was your frame,
I could not leave you with my friends you bore your father's
     name—
I wrapt you in my cotamore at the dead of night unseen,
I heaved a sigh and bade good-bye, to dear old Skibbereen.

Oh, father dear, the day may come when in answer to the call
Each Irishman, with feeling stern, will rally one and all;
I'll be the man to lead the van beneath the flag so green,
When loud and high we'll raise the cry—"Remember Skibbereen!"

Songs of True Love (Mostly Sad)

Shuile Agra

Anonymous

*Eighteenth-century ballad associated with service in European armies
with residual Irish in the title and the first and last lines of the
refrain. There are many versions since it is easily adaptable to
particular places—the Brandon Hill named here is often changed.
The title means literally, "Walk, love," and the almost buried Irish
of the last lines means, "May my darling travel safely."*

As I roved through my new garden bowers,
To gaze upon the fast fading flowers,
And think upon the happiest hours
That fled in Summer's bloom.

Shuile, shuile, shuile agra,
Time alone can ease my woe;
Since the lad of my heart from me did go
Gotheen mavourneen slaun.

'Tis often I sat on my true-love's knee
And many a fond story he told me.
He told me things that ne'er should be.
Gotheen mavourneen slaun.
Shuile, shuile, etc.

I'll sell my rock, I'll sell my reel,
When flax is spun I'll sell my wheel,
To buy my love a sword of steel,
Gotheen mavourneen slaun.
Shuile, shuile, etc.

I'll dye my petticoat, I'll dye it red
And round the world I'll beg my bread,
That all my friends should wish me dead.
Gotheen mavourneen slaun.
Shuile, shuile, etc.

I wish I were on Brandon Hill
'Tis there I'll sit and cry my fill,
That every tear would turn a mill
Gotheen mavourneen slaun.
Shuile, shuile, etc.

No more am I that blooming maid,
That used to rove the valley shade,
My youth and bloom are all decayed,
Gotheen mavourneen slaun.

Shuile, Shuile, Shuile agra,
Time alone can ease my woe;
Since the lad of my heart from me did go
Gotheen mavourneen slaun.

THE BONNY BOY

Anonymous

*Known in England and Scotland as "The Trees They Grow So High,"
this ballad may be based on the marriage in 1631 of the juvenile
laird of Craigton to a girl several years older than he and sung on his
death three years later.*

The trees are growing tall my love,
The grass is growing green
And many's the cruel and bitter day
That I alone have seen
It is a cruel and bitter night
That I must lie alone
Oh, the bonny's boy was young
But was growing.

Oh Father, my father, indeed
You did me wrong
For to go and get me married
To one who is so young
He being only sixteen years
And I being twenty-one
He's a bonny boy, but young—
And still growing.

My daughter, my daughter
I did not do you wrong
For to go and get you married
To one who is so young
He will be a match for you
When I am dead and gone
He's a bonny boy, he's young—
But he's growing.

Oh Father, my father,
I'll tell you what I'll do
I'll send my love to college
For another year or two
And all around his college cap
I'll tie a ribbon blue
Just to let the ladies know
That he's married.

At evening when strolling
Down by the college wall
You'd see the young collegiates
A playing at the ball
You'd see him in amongst them there
The fairest of them all
He's my bonny boy, he's young
But he's growing.

At the early age of sixteen years
He was a married man,
At seventeen the father of
A darling baby son
At eighteen years—t'was over—
O'er his grave the grass grew strong,
Cruel death put an end
To his growing.

I will buy my love a shroud
Of the ornamental brown
And whilst they are making it
My tears they will run down
That once I had a true love
But now he is gone
And I'll mind his bonny boy—
While he's growing.

THE DAWNING OF THE DAY

Anonymous

English rendering of Fainne Geal an Lae, *one of the late eighteenth-century* Dánta Grá. *The title in time came to have a political significance as the occasion of Ireland's freedom from oppression, the dawning of the day following upon the rising of the moon.*

At early dawn I once had been,
Where Lene's blue waters flow,
When summer bid the groves be green,
The lamp of light to glow,
As on by bow'r and town and tow'r,
And wide spread fields I stray,
I met a maid in the green-wood shade,
At the dawning of the day.

Her feet and beauteous head were bare,
No mantle fair she wore,
But down her waist fell golden hair
That swept the tall grass o'er,
With milking pail she sought the vale,
And bright her charms display,
Outshining far the morning star,
At the dawning of the day.

Beside me sat that maid divine,
Where grassy banks outspread,
"Oh! let me call thee ever mine,
Dear maid," I gently said,
A blush o'er-spread her lily cheek,
She rose and sprang away,
The sun's first light pursued her flight
At the dawning of the day.

Cailín Deas Crúite na mBó
(The Pretty Milkmaid)

Anonymous

Known in the nineteenth-century as "The Pretty Milkmaid," it was used by the wily old playsmith Boucicault to ease the dramatic tension in The Colleen Bawn, *and emigrated to America to be one of George M Cohan's songs in his Broadway show* Little Nelly Kelly.

It was on a fine summer's morning,
When the birds sweetly tuned on each bow,
I heard a fair maid sing most charming.
As she sat a-milking her cow;
Her voice it was chanting melodious,
She left me scarce able to go,
My heart it is soothed in solace,
My Cailín deas crúite na mBó.

With courtesy I did salute her,
"Good-morrow most amiable maid,
I'm your captive slave for the future."
"Kind sir, do not banter," she said,
"I'm not such a precious rare jewel,
That I should enamour you so,
I am but a plain country girl,"
Says Cailín deas crúite na mBó.

"The Indies afford no such jewels,
So precious and transparently fair,
Oh! do not to my flame add fuel,
But consent for to love me my dear,
Take pity and grant my desire,
And leave me no longer in woe,
Oh! love me or else I'll expire,
Sweet Cailín deas cruíte na mBó.

"Or had I the wealth of great Damer,
Or all on the African shore,
Or had I great Devonshire treasure,
Or had I ten thousand times more,
Or had I the lamp of Aladdin,
Or had I his genie also,
I'd rather live poor on a mountain,
With Cailín deas cruíte na mBó."

"I beg you'll withdraw and don't tease me
I cannot consent unto thee,
I like to live single and airy,
Till more of the world I do see,
New cares they would me embarrass
Besides, sir, my fortune is low,
Until I get rich I'll not marry,"
Says Cailín deas cruíte na mBó.

"An old maid is like an old almanack,
Quite useless when once out of date,
If her ware is not sold in the morning
At noon it must fall to low rate,
The fragrance of May is soon over,
The rose loses its beauty you know,
All bloom is consumed in October,
Sweet Cailín deas cruíte na mBó."

"A young maid is like a ship sailing,
There's no knowing how long she may steer,
For with every blast she's in danger,
Oh consent love and banish all care,
For riches I care not a farthing,
Your affection I want and no more
In comfort I'd wish to enjoy you,
My Cailín deas cruíte na mBó."

I Know Where I'm Going

Anonymous

A ballad on the often used theme of "the world well lost." It has its most poignant Gaelic version in "Caiseal Mumhan" which begins, "Phosfainn thú gan bha, gan phunt gan áireamh spré," but this is so elegant as to count as a drawing-room ballad.

I know where I'm going,
I know who's going with me,
I know who I love,
But the dear knows who I'll marry.

I'll have stockings of silk,
Shoes of fine green leather,
Combs to buckle my hair
And a ring for every finger.

Feather beds are soft,
Painted rooms are bonny;
But I'd leave them all
To go with my love Johnny.

Some say he's dark,
I say he's bonny,
He's the flower of them all
My handsome, coaxing Johnny.

I know where I'm going,
I know who's going with me,
I know who I love,
But the dear knows who I'll marry.

The Spinning Wheel

John Francis Waller

A love ballad that wedded to its music has some of the musicality of Lieder *and yet can be sung in an equally affecting way in the native mode.*

Mellow the moonlight to shine is beginning,
Close by the window young Eileen is spinning;
Bent o'er the fire her blind grandmother, sitting,
Is crooning and moaning and drowsily knitting.

Chorus
Merrily, cheerily, noiselessly, whirring,
Swings the wheel, spins the wheel, while the foot's stirring,
Sprightly and brightly and airily ringing
Thrills the sweet voice of the young maiden singing.

"Eileen, a chara, I hear someone tapping,"
"'Tis the ivy, dear mother, against the glass flapping,"
"Eily, I surely hear somebody sighing,"
"'Tis the sound, mother dear, of the summer winds dying."
Chorus

"What's that noise that I hear at the window, I wonder?"
"'Tis the little birds chirping the holly-bush under,"
"What makes you be shoving and moving your stool on?
"And singing all wrong that old song of 'The Coolin'?"
Chorus

There's a form at the casement, the form of her true love,
And he whispers with face bent "I'm waiting for you, love,
Get up on the stool, through the lattice step lightly,
We'll rove in the grove while the moon's shining brightly."
Chorus

The maid shakes her head, on her lips lays her fingers,
Steals up from her seat, longs to go and yet lingers;
A frightened glance turns to her drowsy grandmother,
Puts one foot on the stool, spins the wheel with the other.
Chorus

Lazily, easily, swings now the wheel round,
Slowly and lowly is heard now the reel's sound;
Noiseless and light to the lattice above her
The maid steps, then leaps to the arms of her lover.
Chorus

Slower, and slower, and slower the wheel swings,
Lower, and lower, and lower the reel rings;
Ere the reel and the wheel stopped their ringing and moving,
Through the grove the young lovers by moonlight are roving.

TEDDY O'NEILL

Anonymous

*Originally a music-hall song probably of English origin which the
Irish took happily to themselves.*

I dreamt last night, och! bad cess to my dreaming,
I'd die if I thought 'twould come surely to pass;
I dreamt while the tears down my pillow were streaming,
That Teddy was courting another fair lass.
Och! Didn't I wake with the weeping and wailing,
The pain of the thought was too deep to conceal;
My mother cried: "Norah, child, what is your ailing?"
But all I could answer was: "Teddy O'Neill."

I've seen the old cabin beyond the wee boreen,
I've seen the old crossroads where we used to dance;
I've rambled the lanes where he called me his storeen,
And my girlish heart felt the thrill of romance
But now all around is so sad and so dreary,
All dark and all silent, no piper, no reel;
Not even the sun through the casement shines cheery,
Since I lost my heart's darling boy, Teddy O'Neill.

Shall I ever forget when the big ship was ready,
And the moment was come for my love to depart;
How I sobbed like a child: "Och! Goodbye to you, Teddy;"
With a tear on my cheek and a stone in my heart.
He said 'twas to better his fate he went roving,
But what would be gold to the joy I should feel—
If he'd only come back to be tender and loving,
Still poor but my own darling Terry O'Neill.

CARRIGDHOUN
(LAMENT OF THE IRISH MAIDEN)

Denny Lane

Like Shuile Agra, a lament for a latter-day "wild goose." It was written like so many other ballads for The Nation.

> The heath was green in Carrigdhoun,
> Bright shone the sun on Ardnalee,
> The dark green trees bent trembling down,
> To kiss the slumbering Owenabwee,
> That happy day, 'twas but last May,
> 'Tis like a dream to me,
> When Domhnal swore aye, o'er and o'er,
> We'll part no more astor mo chroidhe.

> On Carrigdhoun the heath is brown,
> The clouds are dark over Ardnalee,
> And many a stream comes rushing down
> To swell the angry Owenabwee.
> The moaning blast is sweeping fast
> Thru' many a leafless tree,
> And I'm alone, for he is gone,
> My hawk is flown, ochone machree!

> Soft April showers and bright May flowers
> Will bring the summer back again;
> But will they bring me back the hours
> I spent with my brave Domhnal then?
> 'Tis but a chance, for he's gone to France
> To wear the fleur-de-lis;
> But I'll follow you, my Domhnal dhu,
> For still I'm true to you, a chroidhe.

IF I WERE A BLACKBIRD

Anonymous

Twentieth-century Dublin ballad, popular with a variety of artistes and many street-singers but generally regarded as the property of Delia Murphy.

If I were a blackbird, I'd whistle and sing
And I'd follow the ship that my true love sails in,
And on the top riggings I'd there build my nest,
And I'd pillow my head on his lily white breast.

I am a young maiden and my story is sad
For once I was courted by a brave sailor lad.
He courted me strongly by night and by day,
But now my dear sailor is gone far away.
Chorus

He promised to take me to Donnybrook fair
To buy me red ribbons to bind up my hair.
And when he'd return from the ocean so wide,
He'd take me and make me his own loving bride.
Chorus

His parents they slight me and will not agree
That I and my sailor boy married should be.
But when he comes home I will greet him with joy
And I'll take to my bosom my dear sailor boy.
Chorus

Sports and Other
Enthertainments

THE RAKES OF MALLOW

Anonymous

Mallow, which is set on the north side of the beautiful Blackwater, was a popular resort for the Anglo-Irish gentry of Cork in the eighteenth and early nineteenth century. It was a great centre for hunting and other sports and had its own racecourse. The opportunities for rakishness were considerable.

Beauing, belling, dancing, drinking,
Breaking windows, damning, sinking,
Ever raking, never thinking,
Live the rakes of Mallow.

Spending faster than it comes,
Beating waiters, bailiffs, duns,
Bacchus' true begotten sons,
Live the rakes of Mallow.

One time naught but claret drinking,
Then like politicians, thinking,
To raise the sinking funds when sinking,
Live the rakes of Mallow.

When at home with dada dying,
Still for Mallow-water crying,
But where there is good claret plying
Live the rakes of Mallow.

Living short, but merry lives,
Going where the devil drives,
Having sweethearts, but no wives,
Live the rakes of Mallow.

Racking tenants, stewards teasing,
Swiftly spending, slowly raising,
Wishing to spend all their days in
Raking, as at Mallow.

Then to end this raking life,
They get sober, take a wife,
Ever after live in strife,
And wish again for Mallow.

The Holy Ground

Anonymous

Whether set in Queenstown, as every Cork person will swear (and boy, can they swear!) or in Swansea, look you, or on Manhattan's East River, the ground was far from holy—it was a insalubrious waterfront dive, however fine the girls.

Adieu my fair young maiden,
Ten thousand times adieu,
We must bid good bye to the Holy Ground,
And the girls that we love true,
We will sail the salt sea over,
And return again for sure,
To seek the girls who wait for us,
In the Holy Ground once more,
For the girl I do adore,
And still I live in hopes to see,
The Holy Ground once more.

(Spoken)   Fine girl you are!

Oh the night was dark and stormy,
You scarce could see the moon,
And our good old ship was tossed about,
And her rigging all was torn:
With her seams agape and leaky,
With her timbers dozed and old,
And still I lived in hopes to see,
The Holy Ground once more,
You're the girl I do adore
And still I live in hopes to see,
The Holy Ground once more.
Fine Girl You Are.

And now the storm is over,
And we are safe on shore,
Let us drink a health to the Holy Ground
And the girls that we adore:
We will drink strong ale and porter
Till we make the tap room roar
And when our money all is spent
We will go to sea for more.
You're the girl I do adore
And still I live in hopes to see,
The Holy Ground once more.
FINE GIRL YOU ARE!

Garryowen

Anonymous

Ballad salute to Limerick's most famous suburb and its lively lads. The "Spa" in the first verse refers to the fashionable nineteenth-century practice of drinking water naturally impregnated with sulphur and chalybeate from spa-wells.

Let Bacchus's sons be not dismayed,
But join with me each jovial blade;
Come booze and sing, and lend your aid
To help me with the chorus:—
Instead of Spa we'll drink brown ale,
And pay the reckoning on the nail;
No man for debt shall go to jail
From Garryowen in glory!

We are the boys that take delight in
Smashing the Limerick lamps when lighting,
Through the streets like sporters fighting
And tearing all before us.
Instead, etc.

We'll break windows, we'll break doors,
The watch knock down by threes and fours;
Then let the doctors work their cures,
And tinker up our bruises.
Instead, etc.

We'll beat the bailiffs out of fun,
We'll make the mayor and sheriffs run,
We are the boys no man dares dun,
If he regards a whole skin.
Instead, etc.

Our hearts, so stout, have got us fame,
For soon 'tis known from whence we came;
Where'er we go they dread the name,
Of Garryowen in glory.
Instead, etc.

Johnny Connell's tall and straight,
And in his limbs he is complete;
He'll pitch a bar of any weight,
From Garryowen to Thomond Gate.
Instead, etc.

Garryowen is gone to wrack
Since Johnny Connell went to Cork,
Though Darby O'Brien leaped over the dock,
In spite of all the soliders.
Instead, etc.

Finnegan's Wake

Anonymous

Probably of American origin but sufficiently current in Ireland at the turn of the century to have become, without its apostrophe, the name of one of the country's most notorious if not most read books.

Tim Finnegan liv'd in Walkin Street
A gentleman Irish mighty odd.
He had a tongue both rich and sweet,
An' to rise in the world he carried a hod,
Now Tim had a sort of a tipplin' way
With the love of the liquor he was born,
An' to help him on with his work each day,
He'd a drop of the craythur ev'ry morn.

Chorus
Whack folthedah, dance to your partner
Welt the flure yer trotters shake,
Wasn't it the truth I told you,
Lots of fun at Finnegan's Wake.

One morning Tim was rather full,
His head felt heavy which made him shake,
He fell from the ladder and broke his skull,
So they carried him home his corpse to wake,
They rolled him up in a nice clean sheet,
And laid him out upon the bed,
With a gallon of whiskey at his feet,
And a barrel of porter at his head.

His friends assembled at the wake,
And Mrs. Finnegan called for lunch,
First they brought in tay and cake,
Then pipes, tobacco, and whiskey punch.
Miss Biddy O'Brien began to cry,
"Such a neat clean corpse, did you ever see,
Arrah, Tim avourneen, why did you die?"
"Ah, hould your gab," said Paddy McGee.

Then Biddy O'Connor took up the job,
"Biddy," says she, "you're wrong, I'm sure,"
But Biddy gave her a belt in the gob,
And left her sprawling on the floor;
Oh, then the war did soon enrage;
'Twas woman to woman and man to man,
Shillelagh law did all engage,
And a row and a ruction soon began.

Then Micky Maloney raised his head,
When a noggin of whiskey flew at him,
It missed and falling on the bed,
The liquor scattered over Tim;
Bedad he revives, see how he rises,
And Timothy rising from the bed,
Says, "Whirl your liquor round like blazes,
Thanam o'n dhoul, do ye think I'm dead?"

LANIGAN'S BALL

Anonymous

Athy ballad dating from the sixties of the last century and taken to have been based on an actual rough evening near the town.

In the town of Athy one Jeremy Lanigan
Battered away till he hadn't a pound,
His father he died and made him a man again,
Left him a farm and ten acres of ground,
He gave a grand party to friends and relations,
Who did not forget him when come to the wall,
and if you but listen, I'll make your eyes glisten,
At the rows and ructions of Lanigan's Ball.

Myself to be sure got free invitations,
For all the nice girls and boys I might ask.
And just in a minute both friends and relations,
Were dancing as merry as bees round a cask.
Miss Judy O'Daly that nice little milliner,
Tipped me the wink for to give her a call
And soon I arrived with Peggy McGilligan,
Just in time for Lanigan's ball.

There was lashings of punch and wine for the ladies
Potatoes and cakes there was bacon and tea,
There were the Nolans, Dolans, O'Gradys
Courting the girls and dancing away
The songs they went round as plenty as water,
From the Harp that once sounded in Tara's old Hall,
To sweet Nelly Gray and the Rat-catcher's daughter,
All singing together at Lanigan's ball.

They were doing all kinds
All round the room in a whirl
But Julia and I soon banished the
And tipped them a twist of a real Irish
Och mavrone, how the girls they got ma
And danced till you'd think the ceilings wou
For I spent three weeks at Brooks's Academy,
Learning steps for Lanigan's Ball.

The boys were as merry the girls all hearty.
Dancing away in couples and groups
Till an accident happened young Terence Mccarthy,
He put his right leg through Miss Finerty's hoops.
The creature she fainted and cried "Meelia murther"
Called for her brothers and gathered them all
Carmody swore that he'd go no further
Till he'd have satisfaction at Lanigan's ball.

In the midst of the row Miss Kerrigan fainted
Her cheeks at the same time as red as the rose,
Some of the lads decreed she was painted,
She took a small drop too much I suppose,
Her sweetheart Ned Morgan so powerful and able
When he saw his fair colleen stretched by the wall,
He tore the left leg from under the table,
And smashed all the chaneys at Lanigan's ball.

oys, oh boys, 'tis then there was ructions,
Myself got a lick from big Phelim McHugh,
But soon I replied to his kind introduction,
And kicked up a terrible hullabaloo.
Ould Casey the piper was near being strangled,
They squeezed up his pipes, bellows, chanters and all,
The girls in their ribbons they all got entangled,
And that put an end to Lanigan's ball.

THE ROCKY ROAD TO DUBLIN

Anonymous

*A song with a tune that is popular with instrumentalists and a title
that had become proverbial by the turn of the century.*

In the merry month of May from my home I started,
Left the girls of Tuam nearly broken hearted,
Saluted father dear kissed my darlin' mother
Drank a pint of beer, my grief and tears to smother,
Then off to reap the corn, and leave where I was born,
I cut a stout black-thorn, to banish ghost and goblin,
In a bran new pair of brogues, I rattled o'er the bogs,
And frightened all the dogs on the Rocky road to Dublin.

Chorus
One, two, three,four,five, Hunt the hare and turn her
Down the rocky road and all the ways to Dublin,
Whack fol-lol-de-ra.

In Mullingar that night I rested limbs so weary,
Started by daylight next mornin' light and airy,
Took a drop of the pure, to keep my heart from sinkin',
That's an Irishman's cure, whene'er he's on for drinking.
To see the lasses smile, laughing all the while,
At my curious style, 'twould set your heart a-bubblin'.
They ax'd if I was hired, the wages I required,
Till I was almost tired of the rocky road to Dublin.

In Dublin next arrived, I thought it such a pity,
To be so soon deprived a view of that fine city.
Then I took a stroll all among the quality,
My bundle it was stole in a neat locality;
Something crossed my mind, then I looked behind
No bundle could I find upon my stick a wobblin'.
Enquirin' for the rogue, they said my Connacht brogue,
Wasn't much in vogue on the rocky road to Dublin.

From there I got away, my spirits never failin'
Landed on the quay as the ship was sailin';
Captain at me roared, said that no room had he,
When I jumped aboard, a cabin found for Paddy,
Down among the pigs; I played some funny rigs,
Danced some hearty jigs, the water round me bubblin'
When off Holyhead, I wished myself was dead,
Or better far instead, on the rocky road to Dublin.

The boys of Liverpool, when we safely landed,
Called myself a fool, I could no longer stand it;
Blood began to boil, temper I was losin'
Poor ould Erin's isle they began abusin',
"Hurrah my soul," sez I, my shillelagh I let fly;
Some Galway boys were by, saw I was a hobble in,
Then with a loud hurray, they joined in the affray.
We quickly cleared the way, for the rocky road to Dublin.

There's Whiskey in the Jar

Anonymous

Lively antique song about crime and betrayal from Munster.

As I was going over the far fam'd Kerry mountain
I met with Captain Farrell and his money he was counting,
I first produced my pistol and I then produced my rapier
Sayin' "Stand and deliver for you are my bold deceiver."

Chorus
O, Whack fol the diddle, O,
Whack fol the diddle, O
There's whiskey in the jar
O, Whack fol the diddle, O,
Whack fol the diddle, O
There's whiskey in the jar

He counted out his money and it made a pretty penny
I put it in my pocket and I gave it to my Jenny
She sighed and she swore that she never would betray me
But the devil take the women for they never can be easy.
Chorus

I went into my chamber all for to take a slumber
I dreamt of gold and jewels and for sure it was no wonder
But Jenny drew my charges and she filled them up with water
An' she sent for Captain Farrell, to be ready for the slaughter.
Chorus

And 'twas early in the morning before I rose to travel,
Up comes a band of footmen and likewise Captain Farrell;
I then produced my pistol, for she stole away my rapier
But I couldn't shoot the water so a prisoner I was taken.
Chorus

And if any one can aid me 'tis my brother in the army
If I could learn his station, in Cork or in Killarney.
And if he'd come and join me we'd go roving in Kilkenny
I'll engage he'd treat me fairer than my darling sporting Jenny.
Chorus

A BALLAD OF MASTER MCGRATH

Anonymous

*The great greyhound won the Waterloo Cup in 1868, 1869 and
1871 and was only once beaten. It is celebrated by a memorial
(erected in 1873) at Ballymacmague crossroads three miles from
Dungarvan, Co Waterford.*

Eighteen sixty-nine being the date of the year
Those Waterloo sportsmen and more did appear
For to gain the great prizes and bear them awa'
Never counting on Ireland and Master McGrath.

On the 12th of December, that day of renown,
McGrath and his keeper they left Lurgan town;
A gale in the Channel, it soon drove them o'er,
On the thirteenth they landed on fair England's shore.

And when they arrived there in big London Town,
Those great English sportsmen they all gathered round—
And some of the gentlemen gave a "Ha! Ha!"
Saying: "Is that the great dog you call Master McGrath?"

And one of those gentlemen standing around
Says: "I don't care a damn for your Irish greyhound";
And another he laughs with a scornful "Ha! Ha!"
We'll soon humble the pride of your Master McGrath."

Then Lord Lurgan came forward and said: "Gentlemen,
If there's any amongst you has money to spend—
For you nobles of England I don't care a straw—
Here's five thousand to one upon Master McGrath."

Then McGrath he looked up and he wagged his old tail,
Informing his lordship, "I know what you mane,
Don't fear, noble Brownlow, don't fear them agra,
For I'll tarnish their laurels," says Master McGrath.

And Rose stood uncovered, the great English pride,
Her master and keeper were close by her side;
They have let her away and the crowd cried: "Hurrah!"
For the pride of all England—and Master McGrath.

As Rose and the Master they both ran along,
"Now I wonder," says Rose, "what took you from your home;
You should have stopped there in your Irish demesne,
And not come to gain laurels on Albion's plain."

"Well, I know," says McGrath, "we have wild heather bogs
But you'll find in old Ireland there's good men and dogs.
Lead on, bold Brittania, give none of your jaw,
Snuff that up your nostrils," says MasterMcGrath.

Then the hare she went on just as swift as the wind
He was sometimes before her and sometimes behind,
Rose gave the first turn according to law;
But the second was given by Master McGrath.

The hare she led on with a wonderful view,
And swift as the wind o'er the green field she flew.
But he jumped on her back and he held up his paw
"Three cheers for old Ireland," says Master McGrath.

THE BOULD THADY QUILL

Anonymous

Ballad celebrating Master Quill who, though hailing from the pleasant country west of Cork city is own brother to the rakes from further up the county. Though this ballad was written at the turn of the century it has a lot of eighteenth-century rakishness about it.

Ye maids of Duhallow who're anxious for courtin'
A word of advice I will give unto ye:—
Proceed to Banteer to the Athletic sportin'
And hand in ye'er names to the club committee
But do not commence any sketch of your progress
'Till a carriage you see comin' over the hill
And down thro' the valleys and hills of Kilcorney
With that Muskerry sportsman, the bould Thady Quill.

Chorus
For Ramblin', for Rovin', for football or sportin',
for emptin' a bowl sure as fast as you'd fill
In all your days scovin' you'd find none so jovial
As the Muskerry sportsman the bould Thady Quill.

Thady was famous in many other places;
At the athletic meeting held out in Cloghroe
He won the long jump without throwing off his braces
Goin' fifty-four feet every sweep he would throw.
At the puttin' of the weight there was a Dublin man foremost,
But Thady outreached him and exceeded him still
And around the whole field rang the wild ringin' chorus
Here's luck to our Hero, the bould Thady Quill.

At the great hurlin' match between Cork and Tipperary
'Twas played in the Park by the Banks of the Lee
Our own darlin' boys were afraid of being baten
So they sent for bould Thady to Ballinagree
He hurled the ball left and right in their faces
And show'd those Tipp'rary boys learnin' and skill
If they came in his way, shure he surely would brain 'em
And the papers were full of the praise of Thade Quill.

In the year '91 before Parnell was taken,
Tade was outrageously breakin' the peace;
He got a light sentence for causin' commotion
And six months hard labour for batin' police.
But in spite of coercion he's still agitatin'—
Ev'ry drop of his life's blood he's willin' to spill
To gain for ould Ireland complete liberation
'Till then there's no rest for me bould Thady Quill.

At the Cork Exhibition there was a fair lady,
Whose fortune exceeded a million or more;
But a bad constitution had ruined her completely
And medical treatment had failed o'er and o'er.
"Oh, Mama," said she, "I know what'll cure me
And all me diseases most certainly kill
Give over your doctors and medical tratement
I'd rather one shake outa bould Thady Quill."

Biographical Index

Teresa Brayton was born Teresa Boylan at Kilbrook, near Cloncurry in Co Kildare, in 1868 and qualified as a teacher. She emigrated to America when she was twenty and later wrote poems under the pseudonym T B Kilbrook. She remained a fervent nationalist and knew the 1916 leaders. She married Richard Brayton, and perhaps affected by the nostalgia of her most famous ballad "The Old Bog Road" returned to live in Ireland in the twenties and died in Bray.

Ethna Carbery (Anna Johnston) was born in Ballymena in 1866. She and Alice Milligan edited the Belfast republican journal the *Sean Van Vocht*. She married Seumas MacManus, the folklorist and storyteller from Mountcharles, Co Donegal in 1902 but died soon afterwards. Her poetry with that of her husband and partner was published in a composite volume called *We Sang for Ireland* (1902).

John Keegan Casey was born in Mullingar in 1846, the son of a peasant farmer. He had his first poem published in the *Nation* when he was sixteen and about this time joined the Fenians. He was imprisoned at the age of twenty and became tubercular as a result of harsh prison conditions. He worked as a journalist in Dublin and was a regular contributor to the *Nation* using the pen-name Leo. He died as the result of a traffic accident on Carlisle Bridge, Dublin in 1870.

Thomas Osborne Davis, the founder of the Young Ireland movement, was born in Fermoy in 1814. He became a nationalist while studying law at Trinity, an enthusiast for the Irish language and with Charles Gavan Duffy and John Blake Dillon the educator of O'Connell's emancipated peasantry. Their main medium was the *Nation* and in it they under Davis's guidance established the basis of Irish nationhood. He died of scarlet fever in 1845.

Francis Arthur Fahy was born in Kinvara, Co Galway in 1854. He joined the civil service in 1873 and became president of the London branch of the Gaelic League. He is best known for such songs as "The Donovans" and "The Ould Plaid Shawl" but he was a tireless educator of the children of Irish exiles, reminding them of the glories of their heritage. He died in Clapham in 1935.

Robert Dwyer Joyce was born in Glenosheen, Co Limerick, in 1830. He became first a teacher and then a doctor, graduating from the Queen's College, Cork in 1865. He was professor of English literature at Newman's Catholic University. He left Ireland after the failure of the Fenian agitation and practised medicine in Boston. He returned home in 1883 and died the same year.

Peadar Kearney, the author of Ireland's national anthem, was born in Dublin in 1883 and worked as a cycle-mechanic and a housepainter but his main love was theatre. He wrote many songs serious and comic about the awakening country and left his job at the Abbey to fight in 1916. He was interned in 1920 and after the civil war in which he took the Treaty side retired to obscurity and decorating. He died in 1942.

William Keneally was born in Cloyne, Co Cork in 1828 and was a journalist all his working life. He edited papers in Tipperary and finally settled in Kilkenny, where he served a term as mayor. He published verse under the pseudonym of William of Munster and died in 1876.

Charles Joseph Kickham was born in Mullinahone, Co Tipperary, in 1828. He was intended for medicine but an accident with a pistol when he was thirteen left him deaf and half-blind. He became a journalist and an active Fenian and was sentenced to fourteen years' imprisonment in 1865. He was unable to withstand the usual treatment meted out by warders to political prisoners and was released almost totally blind and in chronic ill-health four years later. He wrote his famous book *Knocknagow* in 1879 and died at Blackrock, Co Dublin in 1882.

Denny Lane was born in Cork in 1818, the son of a distillery owner. He contributed some verse to the *Nation* but his main occupation was as an engineer, with particular interest in the new means of light and heat, gas. He died in 1899 having been sometime president of the Institute of Gas Engineers of Great Britain.

Edward Lysaght was born in Co Clare in 1763 and was a member of the Irish and the English Bars. He was an Irish Volunteer, a friend of Grattan and Curran, and one of the Dublin wits who used a fine satirical sense to attack the Act of Union at every opportunity. Known universally as "Pleasant Ned Lysaght" he may or may not have been the author of "Kitty of Coleraine." He died in 1810.

Thomas Maguire is known only as an itinerant broadsheet seller who wrote the deathless ballad, "Bold Robert Emmet." Facts about his life are scarce but he and his wife were reported in the papers as having been charged with obstruction in London in 1907.

William McBurney was born in Co Down in 1844 and contributed "The Croppy Boy," the song for which he is known, to the *Nation* before emigrating to America and a career of journalism. He wrote under the name of Carroll Malone and died in Boston in 1892.

Patrick Joseph McCall was born in Dublin in 1861 and after education at Newman's university lived mainly by his pen. He may be said to have carried on the work of the *Nation* in his education of the Irish people in their national and cultural heritage. His *Fenian Nights Entertainments* told the heroic stories well but it was such stirring ballads of 1798 as "Kelly from Killane" and "Boolavogue" written for the centenary that made his lasting fame. He died in Dublin in 1919.

Michael Joseph McCann, one of many poets of the *Nation,* was born in Galway in 1824. He was a protégé of John MacHale and taught for some time in his seminary in Tuam. A later career as a London journalist involved the editorship of the *Harp*. He died in London in 1883.

Charles Dawson Shanly was born in Dublin in 1811 and educated at Trinity. He became a journalist, emigrated to America and after a successful career as an editor died in Florida in 1875. He is one of two authors credited with the exquisite song "Kitty of Coleraine."(See entry on Edward Lysaght.)

Charlotte Elizabeth Tonna was born in Norwich in 1790, the daughter of a clergyman. She lived for most of her life in Kilkenny and became a kind of laureate of the Protestant cause though her main literary output was of religious pamphlets written for the Dublin Tracts Society. She died in Kilkenny in 1846.

John Francis Waller was born in Limerick in 1809 and after graduation from Trinity served for some years at the Irish Bar and then took up a career of journalism. He succeeded Charles Lever as editor of the *Dublin University Magazine* and wrote many of the entries of *The Imperial Dictionary of Universal Biography*. He died in Bishop's Stortford, Hertfordshire, in 1894.

Thomas 1st Marquis Wharton was born in 1648 and as a leading Whig was rewarded with the Lord-lieutenantship of Ireland in 1710. He was made marquis in the year of his death, 1714.

Index